Those in Ivory Towers

Those in Ivory Towers

Lawmakers Lawbreakers

Jan Ernest Gainswothy

Copyright © 2018 by Jan Ernest Gainswothy.

ISBN:	Softcover	978-1-5434-0924-6
	eBook	978-1-5434-0923-9

All rights reserved. No part of this book may be reproduced or transmitted in any form or by any means, electronic or mechanical, including photocopying, recording, or by any information storage and retrieval system, without permission in writing from the copyright owner.

Any people depicted in stock imagery provided by Thinkstock are models, and such images are being used for illustrative purposes only.
Certain stock imagery © Getty Images.

Print information available on the last page.

Rev. date: 05/28/2018

To order additional copies of this book, contact:
Xlibris
1-800-455-039
www.Xlibris.com.au
Orders@Xlibris.com.au
777627

CONTENTS

Preface vii

Chapter 1 Suspended in Time 1
Chapter 2 The Wheel of Fortune 21
Chapter 3 Recriminations: A Different Perspective 37
Chapter 4 Stonewalled 49
Chapter 5 From a Death, New Beginnings 59
Chapter 6 Unicameralism 63
Chapter 7 The Now and Where To? 73
Chapter 8 Ivory Towers and Glass Houses 81
Chapter 9 The Brutal Truth and My Disclaimer 93
Chapter 10 Savagery, Sleight of Hand, and Silence 101
Chapter 11 From Pillar to Post: The Last Hoorah 109
Chapter 12 Death the Leveller 123

Epilogue 129
Appendix I 133
Acknowledgements 135

PREFACE

From the planning and the draft of *Without Prejudice:* Nailing the Standard, there was always to be a sequel, although untitled at that stage. This sequel, *Those in Ivory Towers: Lawmakers Lawbreakers*, is the unfinished business of nailing the standard, revealing the legal system to be entrenched with apprehended bias; prejudice.

As a brief background for the new reader, Queensland is a state in the Federation of Australia, which is governed by the Westminster rules of the Crown. Australia, where my legal dramas unfolded, is a Commonwealth nation like Canada, England, and New Zealand.

From the thousands of possible outcomes that may eventuate or be willed by imagination and human expectation, what follows in the pages of this book is how the chips fell. So be it.

There is only one standard to be nailed and one authority on earth: That is God's will be done.

Equally, I must accept that natural justice and recompense are dished up as God ordains. We each have a cross to bear. The naked truth is that each of us is responsible for the consequences of our choices made.

Karma: what goes around comes around.

For readers who have yet to come across my prequel *Without Prejudice*, I have included the book's review in order to provide a thumbnail sketch of its intent, and to allude to a logical thread that links this sequel.

My personal saga related in both books had arisen from a failed business investment, which was to loan moneys to a finance company, supposed to be contracted to bring into Australia; Arabian oil moneys, to redistribute as loans funds at an attractive 10 percent per annum flat rate of interest, whereas, at the time the going borrowing rate here was 18 percent, variable.

Without Prejudice, deals with the denial of a most basic legal claim of money owing. My attempts to recover the investment funds from a law firm's trust were choked by individuals of the Queensland legal system. The book details my approaches to the Queensland Law Society, the Crime and Misconduct Commission, and the Australian Parliament.

Detailed, is a claim as plaintiff, and the district court hearing order, to which I had appealed to the Supreme Court and the Australian High Court in Canberra. There too, an appeal to the Privy Council head, Queen Elizabeth II; every lawful approach had been denied until this last petition, which was the action taken from the advices of the Queen's senior correspondent.

The review was headed:

Provocative Book Bares the Author's Tremendous Struggle for Justice

Without Prejudice, Nailing the Standard, is an explosive account of author Jan Ernest Gainsworthy's overwhelming experience with the justice system.

There are many people that have experienced prejudice and the flaws of the country's justice system.

Most of these cases prove that individuals with highly regarded positions of power and trust can contort the law leaving those who are seeking for justice desperate and doubtful. Now, author Jan Ernest Gainsworthy divulges his own untold story of being prescribed and precluded from natural justice in his book, *Without Prejudice, Nailing the Standard.* This book has crystallized from the chronic, ongoing legal experiences of the author, borne from two decades of a personal overwhelming struggle for justice. Many innocent people go to the grave shafted, with no fair affordable legal path to challenge a decision of the legal system.

The book contains explosive details and truth that illustrate how individuals in highly regarded positions of power and trust contort the law. This account is a true story that has been denied the opportunity to put to air. However, behind the contempt for the failing system, and cynicism of the writer, rests the hope of answered prayer.

Informative, stimulating and boldly presents the real situations in the justice system; this book proposes to ignite hope and inspire justice—people power; justice for all, in accordance with there is only one authority on Earth.

Indeed, *Without Prejudice, Nailing the Standard* is an intriguing book that confronts the administration of law and order in the society.

This sequel, *Those in Ivory Towers - Lawmakers Lawbreakers*, picks up the ongoing legal saga at the point where Jan is sitting on the edge of the leather lounge in the federal minister's office, several months prior to yet another disdainful whitewash of a genuine petition to the federal executive of the senate to have this travesty of justice quashed.

All statements contained in this book were made reliant upon the facts at hand. All are expressly told without prejudice.

Dedication of this book goes to a dear friend, Steven R, a.k.a. "the Captain," who passed suddenly, and literally shook my reality.

Seeing Steven's coffin drifting behind two closing sets of curtains while the last post was being played profoundly affected my now and changed my perception, then and there.

The harsh reality of life on earth is that life as we know it in the human form is ephemeral.

It was Steven who had told me, two weeks prior to his sudden parting, "That is how the system has worked since Adam was a boy. Don't take it so seriously, Jan."

Steve's words echo and have served to remind me to stop and smell the flowers; there is far too much joy in the world to be had. Be grateful for your life and health. Money cannot buy either. Do not be bogged down in bloody-mindedness, and remember what Batman is purported to have said: "You cannot live on crime-fighting alone."

There's something in that for everybody.
If you are going to laugh about a situation later, why not do it now?
Live and laugh. For Shirley, laughter is the best medicine.
Please take your medicine: Laugh out loudly!

Jan Ernest Gainsworthy

Prelims

The frontmatter is an addition to this rewritten sequel of *Without Prejudice, Nailing the Standard*. It is an icebreaker, after five-years in the wilderness, to the relaunch my book dedicated to the 'Captain'.

I believe this story also, needs to be told, as further example of community standards unravelling, due to individuals usurping the power of the one authority, solely to stroke their own ego and promote personal gain. The story depicts how individuals assigned to responsible, privileged positions, whom also, incorrectly believe they have autonomous rule, and are above the law; protected by the insular system. Moreover, for the most part, escape the consequences of their indiscretions and their unrulily decisions.

Initially, as the lab technician, I was witness to the BSM, the Business Services Manager, at the institution, where I was stationed, bully the cleaner, L.S., assigned to cleaning duties of my building.

The targeting by the BSM, W. T., of the cleaner L.S., was relentless over a period of two years. W.T. had an extreme personal dislike for L.S., the basis of the targeting and bullying. The BSM would summon L.S. to the principal's office without an agenda. At the meeting with the principal present, W.T. would unleash a barrage of contrived allegations of wrongdoing against the cleaner. As clarification, L.S. had been in the system for ten-years and was regarded as a truly competent cleaner and a model employee of Education Australia. In fact, L.S. was invited to start at the site, because of known work ethic, by the previous BSM, R.A.

The situation turned sour within the first weeks of W.T. starting as an 'acting' BSM. W.T. would be out of depth in a puddle on the campus. W.T. was, from all accounts a teacher's aide or an administration officer, not qualified as a business services manager. My crude acronym for BSM, is *bull shit master*, reasons, which may well become apparent later.

L.S., at wits-end, complained in writing to the principal, T.J.. It took T.J., nine-months to reply buy a single page letter. T.J.'s reply, said: "I have investigated the matter and can find no evidence to support your claim." I was nominated on L.S.'s letter of complaint as witness to the bullying, yet T.J, nor a deputy principal approached as a witness to the complaint matter.

In the meantime, L.S. was stitched up and given a 'code of conduct', for daring to challenge the BSM's authority.

In the winds, it would have been deduced that I had helped L.S. to write a formal complaint. Thence, came the targeting of me, by the 'acting' BSM, W.T..

First, W.T. cut my in-house messages by email, then had an administration officer, take back my lift-fob, on the pretence that the office was short for day-visitors, and new lift-fobs were being ordered. My reliable sources told me that there was a "draw full", and the excuse, contrived. And there were others issued with a lift-fob, such as the groundsman that had no demand to use a lift at all.

Then, in May 2017, I had 20-hours removed from my timesheet overnight. Sunday, I had 60-hours, ADO, Monday morning I had 40-ADO hours.

Knowing the collusion between the BSM and the Principal, I wrote to the deputy principal, M.N. with my concerns and complaint.

Within days, M.N. presented, unannounced, to my prep-room in the science block to relay his verbal reply. The system's modus operandi is that nothing is put on paper, a ploy which eliminates any future comeback of what was actually stated. M.N. told me M.N. had spoken to W.T. and because M.N. had no knowledge of time clocks or timesheets; had given the matter back to the BSM to sort. M.N. was told by the BSM that the loss of 20-hours ADO was a soft-ware glitch across the board, and W.T. was on-to-it. And, with perceived doubt by me, M.N. said, "the lift-fobs have been ordered, 'today'." My intranet messages were restored within 24-hours. Due to a holiday break, the timesheet issue was not address for 3-4 weeks.

W.T., after the time lapse, merely printed off a corrected series of timesheets, with no errors, nor the timesheet I had signed-off on. Realising my no-win circumstance, I signed off on the new batch of timesheets with the missing 20-ADO hours. My thinking was that: "Losing 20-ADO hour, over 20-years was a loss I could absorb. Also,

I had made my point, and the BSM would be on notice not to tamper with my recorded times by the biometric clock.

Ah! It happened again! 20-ADO hours went missing, overnight, in August 2017.

I was initially told it was a soft-ware error.

I then made a formal complaint to my Union, who initially fluffed around and skirted my complaint.

After which, the BSM took away the grace period on the biometric time-clock, from all non-teaching staff.

To this, I wrote to the education minister. This was to begin the cycle of denial. The minister directed my complaint to the director general, who forwarded it to the Northwest Regional Director, N.J. I had known N.J personally, as we had crossed paths at another teaching institution, fifteen years prior. I negotiated a meeting with N.J., by referral from the director general, Education Australia.

I met with N.J., at the NW Regional office, in September 2017, to relay my story and concerns, and requested a "level playing field", when asked what was my desired outcome?

N.J. gave assurances that he would monitor the situation and that I did have rights as an employee of Education Australia. I told N.J. that M.N. had given back my timesheets for the BSM to correct. N.J. responded by saying, "That can't be helpful."

N.J. passed on my complaint to a senior human recourses officer, A.V. and we subsequently met at the Northwest Regional office. I mentioned, I have undertaken these steps to document the complaint, 'for the record', in order to stop the bullying and prevent it happening again.

A.V. confirmed it was now on file. This was after the first loss of ADO-hours.

I complained to A.V. on the second occasion and again approached the Union for assistance. The Union eventually drafted a letter to the Principal, and within 24-hours my second lot of missing hours were returned along with the restoration of the grace period.

For my troubles of recording the breach of code of conduct, and the revengeful nature of W.T., I was targeted; locking me out of the administration building, where the time-clock is situated.

I had for four-years, clocked on at 6:30 am, now at the instruction by the BSM, I was prohibited to clock on before 7:00 am.

I complained to A.V., however, A.V. had been moved on to another post. That's how the system works.

The short story is that I had a meeting to resolve issues with the Director of Human Resources, P.K., and R.S. of the Ethical Standards Unit. The meeting reminded me of being in the dock of the Supreme Court of Appeal, with three judges denying me of any argument.

P.K sent the reply to R.S. to give to me and I responded to R.S.. The following is my take on the ambush. You be the Judge.

Jan Gainsworthy
Lab Technician

11 April 2018

R.S.
Human Resource: Senior Investigator
North West Region
Education Department Australia
PO Box 1392, Aus. 1369

Dear R.S.

I have been invited by the Director, Human Resource, to contact you regarding the outcome of discussion, at our meeting on 27 March 2018.

I had anticipated the white-wash and was waiting to reply to P.K. My views are outlined in the letter to P.K. (See attached)
Firstly, at no point did I make acquiescence. I stand by all I have written. I have no further questions regarding the content of the contrived outcome.

As I have stated, I shall await the outcome of the independent commissioner.

Yours faithfully

Jan Gainsworthy

---

11 April 2018

P.K.
Education Australia
North West Regional Office

Without Prejudice

Dear P.K.

First impressions of your conduct at our meeting, on the 27 March 2018 and in the presence of R.S., I found you to be over zealous and officious.

However, upon re-evaluation of my initial perception and with the benefit of 20/20 hindsight, my now considered opinion of your demeanour at the time is one of which you grossly over-reached your authority. Not flattering of your position as senior human resources officer, there, to resolve my concerns I had recently raised with the department, regarding my workplace.

As senior human resources officer, you gave no regard to my present personal situation, which I explained as my established morning routine for four years. As an educator, I have always worked as a team member of the science department in the best interests of department and student outcomes for all, insuring the best possible, safe, learning environment of the teaching laboratories. Yet, starting early, was my preferred way of covering the required ADO hours for the year and with the exceptional work-load of a first-term, I contend that it was a reasonable approach for all concerned, to request access to the timeclock, prior to 7:00 am.

The change to "housekeeping rules and times" has issues, in that major changes, affecting all staff, need to be ratified by the LCC and clear notification given prior to, so staff with concerns can raise them before the LCC, in order for it to be an administration directive. This is due process of democracy. No one individual has totality rule; the fundamental principle of the Magna Carta, set down 800-years ago.

Further P.K., I was insulted by you referring to me as an "obstinate child" because I did not do my ADOs in the afternoon. For the record, I had accrued nearly 30-ADO hours. And too, I was waiting on a direction from the department in regard to my starting times and had not signed my ADO agreement, which technically meant that I had no agreement.

I take exception to your brutal approach of condemning me for having a negative ADO hour tally and insinuating I had deliberately not worked past my normal hours of employment in the afternoon. Your ill-conceived perception is a furphy, in fact an untruth, as in accordance with a bulletin posted on the 21 March 2018, to all employees, by Henry Jeffreys, deputy Director-General, states clearly the interpretation of the Department, in regard to ADO hours of non-teaching staff. We see from the bulletin:

Can non-teaching employees go into a negative ADO balance?

Yes. However, the ADO Agreement covers the entire 2018 year and should be monitored throughout the year to ensure a zero balance is achieved by year's end.

The above edict from the deputy Director-General, fairly supports my criticism of the email, dated Tuesday, 6 March 2018, from S.D.,

HR Executive officer, at my workplace. In the email that I found most offensive and threating, it was stated that:

> *"As a Department directive – shortfalls in balance will not be carried over to next term and may result in a loss of pay over the holidays."*

This is an outrageous lie! One, in which you P.K., personally condoned and responded to me by saying, *"They were perfectly in their rights to send the email."*

Not so, P.K.. It is at the heart of the corruption.

I had requested to be furnished with the section of the Department's directive which makes the above declaration. According to the deputy Director-General's account no such directive exists.

It is a fabricated bullying tactic by the author, which you approved of.

In regard to the author, I have a reliable source, that was told by S.D., that the said email was contrived by W.T., the BSM.

Also, the statement in another email sent to me by S.D., claiming she had spoken to my HOD, Mr Arthur, about my starting-times, is yet another fabrication of W.T., under the pretext of it being generated by S.D.. It is fraudulent, unethical and unconscionable behaviour of W.T., which you condone.

I approached Mr Arthur for clarification. His reply, *"I don't recall ever speaking to S.D. about the matter."* It was W.T. that had spoken to Mr Arthur.

The creation of the position of HR Executive officer, at the beginning of this year was in response, I believe, to my bullying complaint to N.J.. The position was created to have the appearance that W.T. was precluded from processing and accounting for individual's timesheets. Indeed, it was a cover-up to conceal the theft and attempted theft of my ADO hours, of May & August 2017, respectively.

In fact, W.T. still has ultimate control, veiled by the newly created position. I believe it is a deception condoned by the Regional Director, who failed to protect me from further bullying in my workplace. I have subsequently advised N.J., in writing, and too, A.V., of the escalating bullying situation, however, there has been no response, nor any action undertaken to curtail the unconscionable behaviour of

W.T.. My concerns I had raised in February 2018, were not dealt with individually, nor in a timely manner.

To these facts, I allege N.J. to be culpable for his non-specific performance in protecting and providing me with a safe workplace and has ignored my plea for assistance.

There again, as NW Regional Director, N.J. must have been aware of the meeting and its agenda, set-up by you, with R.S. and myself, on the 27 March 2018. N.J. is surely accountable for your demeanour, as his representative at the particular meeting.

To clarify the issue of the locked administration door; I am not challenging the need for security, and keeping the door locked until 7:00 am. In fact, I had suggested to the present BSM, at the time of the installation of the timeclock, the kitchen door should be locked at all times and a key-pad installed for all staff to have a pin-number for access, which would monitor the coming and going of each individual. The BSM at that threw her hands in the air and said, *"We can't afford that!"*. I made the suggestion based on my personal experience as a shop proprietor and hotelier. The back door is considered a major security risk and needs to be "secured at all times." I make the point: By leaving the door "open" after 7:00 am is fundamentally a flawed security practice. In particular, I see that an agitated, angry parent or guardian could burst through the unsecured door and confront the principal, without any prior warning. On that account alone, the kitchen door should be secured 24/7 and staff given access by a pin-code.

My objection was having been denied access to the timeclock, by only one person's decision. To request to begin work 30-minutes prior to 7:00 am is not an unreasonable request given that I had, I believed, a verbal contract/approval with the employer, through the previous BSM, R.A. and a precedent had been set over the past four-years. One cannot contract out of a contract.

I believe any qualified fair-minded decision maker would grant me access at 6:30 am, given my set of circumstances, and first-term workload. As my response to the unreasonable denial, to give me access to the timeclock prior to 7:00 am, I shall quote Lord Diplock, a Justice of the Privy Council:

> *"So outrageous in its defence of logic or moral standards that no sensible person who had applied his mind to the question to be decided could have arrived at it."*

In regard to the principal's letter to the Union, I found your comments repugnant, echoing the apprehended bias I had flagged previously. I contend the principal's letter was contrived by W.T., the BSM, but the Principal must take responsibility for it and apologise to me.

Again, with the 20-20 vision of hindsight, I presume, with high probability that the meeting you called on the Friday, for the following Tuesday, was at the behest of the NW Regional Director.

I believe it was a knee-jerk reaction from my latest letter to N.J. N.J. has not responded to any of my correspondence since we first met on 12 September 2017. N.J. sent two henchmen to my workplace, to sort the situation at the meeting, you called with the agenda listed as: Complaints lodged, 14 February, 27 February, 14 March & 15 March.

I was taken aback by the breach of meeting protocol, when I was assailed by the first-item on the 'hidden' agenda of a collaborated cowardly attack, of having negative ADO hours. It is axiomatic that you were fed misinformation by the BSM, who had been stalking me by way of scrutinizing my start and finishing times on a daily basis. It was L.C., a cleaner who told me, *"W.T. will be watching your starting times."* It was L.C. that also told me, *"You know you can't start work before seven, Yan."* In fact, I did not know I could not start work before 7:00 am. What I did know was I was locked out of accessing the timeclock before seven.

Also, the lie that non-teaching staff cannot accrue negative ADO hours, needs to be addressed. In fact, at the time of the meeting, I had performed my regular hours of duty over the term and I had accrued a positive balance of 29 ADO hours. (If my missing twenty-ADO hours, from May 2017, were returned; I would have a positive tally of 50 ADO hours.) It was hurtful, when it was suggested I wanted to get paid for ADO hours I had not worked, when that has never been the case, nor my intention, for twenty-years of my employment. I make the point: I am paid at the rate of a 003 – lab tech and perform the duties of a 004.

For the record: I shall state my obdurate stance, succinctly, "I have done nothing wrongly!" There are no consequences for rightful actions.

P.K., as you were representing the minister for Education Australia, the premier, the department of Education Australia (namely the regional director and the director of ethical standards unit) I shall be notifying those individuals, and accordingly insisting that any determination made by yourself to be null and void due to your apprehended bias so flagrantly displayed, and your unprofessional assail on my good character, is unacceptable. You refused to consider my 20-year work history with Education Australia and ignored any effect your belligerent stance would have on my wellbeing, work/life balance.

I have subsequently sought investigation by the independent commissioner, Dr. S. N., though my federal minister of parliament; I shall await the outcome.

Yours sincerely

Jan Gainsworthy

I have labelled the situation as a storm in a teacup. No one has approached me, nor raised the subject of bullying.

The story has been added to compare, as a parallel story, to the ongoing experience dealing with the Queensland legal fraternity. In both, there is one perpetrator, who has had the backing of all those in the systems to deny me justice. These individuals, in highly regarded position, have traded their integrity, to uphold the actions and the lies of the two perpetrators. Rathdowney in the legal system and W.T. in the education system. "If you want to be a 'big fish' you must find a small pond." Thus, we continue from the prequel, in dedication of this book to the 'Captain' Steven R.

CHAPTER 1

Suspended in Time

Scheduled by appointment, I was ushered into the small, plush room of the Bonner federal electoral office at Wynnum, Queensland, and asked if I would like a cup of tea or coffee. I replied, "A glass of water would be fine, thank you." The MP, Vladimir Rossi, and I formally greeted one another, shaking hands and introducing ourselves.

"Please take a seat, Jan," offered Vladimir.

Anxious of the unknown response that would follow; I sat on the edge of the leather lounge opposite my federal member of parliament, with his secretary adjacent, jotting down notes of our meeting.

With a little quiver in my voice, I proceeded to say, "I have an ongoing legal issue regarding monies paid into a solicitor's trust, and to this day, the law firm has not accounted for my funds. I have been to every authority, and I have even written to Her Majesty Queen Elizabeth II, as Her Majesty is the head of the Privy Council. I am here today, on the advice of the queen's senior correspondent, asking for your help. I have put together an affidavit with an indexed, paginated bundle of evidence and priors of two solicitors, Joe Rathdowney and Sean Ruck. I'm respectfully requesting that you table these documents in the Australian Federal Parliament."

The young MP appeared to be genuinely concerned, picking up on my state of heightened anxiety. There was a trace of empathy when Vladimir related to me that his father, Virgil Rossi, had been a Queensland Supreme Court judge. His father also had been mauled by the political/legal systems, which in turn ruined Virgil's reputation and career. Virgil Rossi was the only judge to have been sacked by the Queensland Parliament, after the Fitzgerald Inquiry.

Vladimir Rossi said, "We have a 'gun' barrister on our team who is a senator. Do you mind if I pass these documents on to him?" The senator was the Honourable Bill Gillard, shadow attorney general.

Not being aware of the Honourable Bill Gillard, I shrugged. "Not at all," was my response. "If that is the direction it needs to go, please do."

Vladimir then asked, "Jan, have you written to the state attorney general?"

"Yes. I wrote in the first instance to Mr. Dobbs, the Queensland attorney general, who, through his office, referred me to the federal attorney general, Senator Rupert McCleverland. His office subsequently informed me they could not be of assistance.

"Here is a copy of my affidavit and submissions to the federal executive for Senator Gillard, the barrister, to be tabled in parliament. I have an extra copy for your office."

The minister replied, "There was no need for the second copy because our office could have made another copy."

"That's okay," I said. "I still have two others as backup."

As I rose to my feet, the minister thanked me for having the resilience to come this far. Leaving the office, my final comment was, "What is contained in the documents is explosive. I would be happy to clarify any detail with the barrister."

"More than likely, you will get a call from the senator. Are you able to get to his Brisbane offices if need be?" the MP enquired.

"Certainly. I can jump on a train and be in the heart of the city within an hour or two at most."

The minister politely opened the external door leading to the concrete apron at the front of his office, and I departed.

With my emptied briefcase, I strolled the two blocks to where I was holed up.

Parliament was to sit the following week, and I had an unjustified expectation that in parliament's two-week block of sitting, my affidavit to the Federal Executive Council would be tabled for a review.

I tuned the radio to the live parliamentary sessions. It had been years since I had any interest in the daily affairs of schoolyard politics. I had forgotten that the chair of the House opened each day by reciting the Lord's Prayer. I thought, *Hypocrites! If only they believed and practised what is written in Romans 13.*

By the end of the two weeks of parliament's sitting, I was so disinterested that I chose not to turn the radio on. My expectations of a speedy outcome had vanished too. I was suspended in time, things having moved at a snail's pace.

To console myself, I concluded that the documents in my submission needed to be tested by the barrister for validity before being tabled.

There was still to come a final session of parliament before closing for 2011. Perhaps politically there was a right timing for my affidavit to be tabled.

I held firm to my belief, stated in *Without Prejudice: Nailing the Standard,* that

"I know this to be my last avenue of approach, but I am confident about those into whose hands they were delivered."

My confidence was bolstered by researching on the Internet the senator's first speech, in which I saw alignment with the way I saw the world and the role of government.

The Honourable Senator Gillard began his inaugural speech by alluding to the constitution and remarking on two of our founding fathers, Barton and Deakin. Interestingly, our first two prime ministers, Alfred Deakin and Edmund Barton, were barristers and had served on the bench of the High Court of Australia.

The senator went on to state, "They brought back with them not just a constitution, but all of the hopes, the aspirations and the ideals of both a new nation and a new century."

I was buoyed by his vision of a successful nation: "A successful nation depends upon the spirit of its people. It depends upon the wisdom of its governments. But not least of all, it depends upon its constitutional foundations."

Senator Gillard quoted Sir Isaiah Berlin, whom he regarded as "the greatest liberal philosopher of the twentieth century":

> If the essence of men is that they are autonomous beings, authors of values, of ends in themselves, the ultimate authority which consists precisely in the fact

that they are willed freely, then nothing is worse than to treat them as if they were not autonomous, but, whose choices can be manipulated by their rulers. To treat men in this way is to treat them as if they were not self-determined.

"Nobody may compel me to be happy in this way," said Kant. Paternalism is the greatest despotism imaginable.

This is so because it is to treat men as if they were not free, but human material for me, the benevolent reformer, to mould in accordance with my own, not their, freely adopted purposes … To manipulate men, to propel them toward gaols which you the social reformer see, but they may not, is to deny their human essence, to treat them as objects without wills of their own, and therefore to degrade them.

In his speech, Senator Gillard also pledged: "For as long as I sit in this place I will defend the absolute right of all citizens to the free expression of their opinions, no matter how unfashionable, ignorant or offensive those opinions seem to others."

To me, Jan Ernest Gainsworthy, the senator's pledge was reassuring that my submission to the Australian Parliament through the Federal Executive Council was indeed in the right hands. Bill Gillard's words, I believed, were from his heart. It showed me that Senator Gillard had the integrity, the strength of character, the position, and the legal background as a gun barrister to force out the truth that had been so long buried by those anointed ones of the Queensland legal system.

Finally, after twenty-two years of being prescribed and precluded from natural justice, there was now a ray of hope—an end to my overwhelming struggle to be heard.

I was buoyed by Senator Gillard's standing and the remarks contained within the senator's speech. Another excerpt that galvanised my confidence of a successful outcome follows. The senator stated:

> But of all the obligations of government, perhaps the most fundamental is this, the obligation to protect the weak from the strong. It is a need as old as government

itself, for men first formed themselves into civil society to protect themselves from predators without. They enacted the earliest of all types of law, the criminal law, to protect them from predators within.

Now, having the background of the persons with the carriage of my submission, I wrote a personal, handwritten letter to the federal minister, Vladimir Rossi, to thank him greatly for forwarding my affidavit to the Honourable Senator Bill Gillard and for his determination and action.
The letter, dated October 2011, read:

Dear Vladimir

> Firstly, I am so grateful you allowed me the time and opportunity of meeting with you at your office, regarding my ongoing unconstitutional treatment by the Queensland legal system.
> I have only recently accessed your letter dated 15 September 2011 and I am buoyed by your alacrity to write to me personally and to forward my submission to Senator Gillard.
> I have 'googled' the Senator's background and profile on the net. I am again encouraged by his accomplishments and integrity. Truly, Bill Gillard, the 'gun barrister', is the man that is extremely capable to comprehend and assist with my legal nightmare.
> Many thanks indeed for your personal recommendations.
> I too, followed-up regarding your father and can see how, those with the power in the wrong hands, can cruel the lives of good men, loved by God. "All is well."
> After all these years of over-whelming struggle, it is comforting to know I have the support from true professionals that cannot be cajoled nor manipulated by the system.
> I have to these ends been inspired to write a book; Razorback One - Nailing the Standard.

As part of my research, I would dearly love to meet and have an audience with your father.

Please let me know if you think that would be appropriate? Upon your father's approval, of course.

With extreme gratitude
Sincerely

Jan Ernest Gainsworthy

Indeed, I was prepared to wait with the knowledge that there are no coincidences and my affidavit was in the right hands to ensure a forced truth.

However, the long, enforced waiting was still on. Again, I was suspended in time, with no feedback and only my second-guessing of "What's happening? What are they doing now?"

Had the Hon. Senator Gillard spoken to Rathdowney or Ruck? Had Senator Gillard retrieved the indictments from the Queensland State Archives as verification?

With no communication from Rossi or Gillard, my doubt came creeping back. There had been far too much passage of time with nothing to halt the thought, *What if?*

It was late November, and the federal parliament was sitting for the last time for 2011.

I had hoped I would hear something, anything, within the last two weeks.

Nothing! Silence was the deafening reply, except for a missed phone call from the federal minister's secretary, Monica.

I was returning to the Gold Coast from Melbourne. I was driving through Sodaney on a six-lane freeway, in bumper-to-bumper traffic, again moving at a snail's pace, more like a congested car park. It took me twenty-five minutes to get off and out of the traffic to return Monica's call.

My mind raced: could this be the call I had been waiting for twenty-odd years?

It was five minutes to five o'clock, Queensland time, when I returned the call. The MP's secretary informed me that the senator's office had rung wanting to know if I had another copy of my submissions. Monica requested I post it to her.

I replied, "It's rather a large volume. I will personally deliver it to the electoral office first thing Monday, as I will be back in Wynnum." I asked, "Did the senator's office give any indication as to what's happening?"

"No," she replied. "All I can tell you is that they're looking into it."

"Hmm … I see. I'll be there Monday at nine." And, I hung up.

I was perplexed. Why would the office of the minister request another copy for the senator when they could have made copies from their second copy?

What had happened to the two copies?

I landed at the federal MP's office in Wynnum at 9:00 a.m. sharp to deliver the third copy. I asked the secretary then, "Are there any further developments?"

"No. Thank you for delivering this copy to me. I shall forward it on to the senator," Monica said.

Same, same: more waiting and more second-guessing. What was going on? It appeared they were stalling me. Nothing had transpired. I was suspended in time, once more in a state of inertia. Doubt was snowballing from no communication as to what was going on. My anticipation of a successful outcome before Christmas was subsiding and turning to despair.

Was the once gun barrister Bill Gillard, now politician, avoiding commitment of office?

I had formed the view that once a solicitor, always a solicitor. Could it be that the barrister had returned to the first rules of solicitors and barristers, which were to make no admissions, say nothing, and avoid the truth at all cost?

It appeared that the senator's political agenda was most important, and action, contrary to the solicitor's silent oath, was taboo. It seemed to me too that Senator Gillard, having gone through the system and having been anointed by those within the system with a leg-up, now had his hands tied and was unwilling to proceed with what may well be a political catastrophe for him.

Having been in the high-ranking position of barrister, Gillard would be acquainted with all the players I had named for their non-specific performance. It could be that the people he needed to persuade were the very people who had anointed him and given him the right of passage to be a senator, a leg-up on his high horse.

I did not envy Bill's position, taking into account that Senator Gillard was also an anointed one. He was between a rock and a hard place, yet he must act according to the rules. I believed Bill Gillard must act according to his conscience and his pledge.

I felt it was a moral dilemma for the senator, politically sensitive, but I knew Senator Bill Gillard had to live with the consequences of his choice. Free will: everybody is called, but seldom does anyone heed.

My frustration at bureaucracy was an itch I could not seem to scratch.

Suspended in time by the inertia of the anointed ones and a suppressed, unwilling spirit of my fellow man, I was hamstrung, with no place to go.

Over twenty years of banging my head against the brick wall of the legal system, I have come to a self-diagnosis of chronic existential anxiety.

Existential Anxiety

The condition caused directly from the non-action ("non-action" is my terminology for the refusal (*for eighteen years*) to table the trust account ledger of Rathdowney MacDraw) by the Law Society, the Legal Services Commission, and the Office of the Queensland Ombudsman. This is evidence of the fact that they were protecting Rathdowney and perverting the course of natural justice.

This existential anxiety engendered:

- Plain, ordinary, everyday fear
- Exaggerated fear
- Disappearance of normal securities
- Fear of the "nothing"
- Fear of the future
- Ontological anxiety (relating to the philosophy of existence)

The waiting was excruciating, not knowing when or even if Minister Rossi or Senator Gillard would act.

I waited until the New Year. Then, with a feeling of hopelessness, I wrote to Senator Gillard directly to formally introduce myself. My intention, thinking the letter may well be a prick to his conscience, was to induce action.

Below is the letter:

Dear the Hon. Senator Gillard

Firstly, Happy New Year 2012.

I am Jan Ernest Gainsworthy, a constituent of the Commonwealth, whom my Federal MP, Vladimir Rossi, has introduced you to by letter dated 15 September 2011.

My intent of contacting you personally is to keep abreast of your findings thus far and your prognosis in relation to my Affidavit to the Federal Executive Council and my claim for justice.

Fresh evidence of the defendant's priors would negate all previous determinations.

Senator, I wish to stress that you are the only person privy to these new findings.

I know that these priors that no party has seen have the power to deem the Hearing a mishearing or mistrial.

These Priors have been concealed from all the Courts and Judges. I believe also that had Recovery of Documents been extracted before the Hearing, then there would have been no need for me to go through the lengthy Appeals processes, which also would be deemed mistrials because of the concealed evidence of Mr Rathdowney's priors

Every Court would be unable to make conclusive judgement due to the concealment.

Mr Rathdowney by his actions has brought disrepute to the Legal System.

I know Senator Gillard that you have the authority to force the truths and attain justice, to put an end to my long and enforced waiting that I have had to endure.

Sincere thanks for your considerations.
Yours faithfully

Jan Ernest Gainsworthy

I posted the letter by express mail directly to the senator, addressed *personal and confidential*.

Another anxious waiting period followed, fingers crossed for a forthcoming positive response. I was treading on eggshells, not wanting to p-one-ss the senator off, because he had the capacity and the capability to set things right, or deal me a backlash, as the commissioner, Bob Jenkins, had done in 2007.

However, Senator Gillard's avoidance to act or respond thus far indicated a lack of willingness. There were obviously in his mind no political points to be scored by acting for an outsider who had had his day in court.

I agreed there were no political points the senator could score. It may well tarnish his image with the anointed ones, because Bill had to directly oppose the unwritten, secret law of the legal system, which is to protect their own at all costs. Admit nothing to anyone outside the circle, close the ranks tighter if need be—anything one can muster to avoid revelations of the truth. Cover-up and denial appear to be the well-kept, open secrets of the legal system.

I emailed the minister, Vladimir Rossi, on January 30, expressing in my opinion:

> That nearly five months of further long enforced waiting was sufficient time allowed for you or the Senator to indicate whether, or not you are able to assist me, in regard to my justice claim.

There was clearly a certain amount of frustration evident in my email to the minister. I went on to say:

> I intend not to wait any further as the waiting has a detrimental effect on my health.

Monica, the secretary of Vladimir Rossi, MP, phoned me in early February to get my permission to approach Senator Bill Gillard concerning the developments of my submission to the Federal Executive Council.

I waited a couple of weeks. On 27 February 2012, I emailed the minister directly, commenting as follows:

Dear Sir

> Please pardon the intrusion once more. I had a call from your office a couple of weeks ago and I am anxious to know if anything came of the follow-up, in regard to responses of the Senator' office.
> I have over 22 years been in this situation of waiting and second-guessing.
> If there is nothing that can be done, please tell me.
> Maybe you can suggest someone else that may be able to assist me?
> To me it has far exceeded a reasonable amount of time to wait with no reply
> In addition, I am prepared to move on but would like a definite yes OR no.
>
> Many thanks for your consideration.
> Yours sincerely
>
> Jan Ernest Gainsworthy

A month later, still neither acknowledgement nor reply.

After months of being suspended in time, what would any reasonable person assume, having not had a reply from either office?

From my initial meeting with the minister, it was now, in total, an extended seven month wait with not even a courteous reply. Further, there was no repugnant retort. An absolute no was likewise not forthcoming from my prompting letter and email.

It was seven months of royal silence because what I was asking was seemingly now in the too-hard basket. Perhaps Vladimir Rossi, MP, regretted showing a little human concern and readily offering the services of their team's gun barrister, Bill Gillard.

There may well have been a breakdown of communication between their offices due to Rossi's alacrity in putting the barrister on the spot without notice. I sensed there may be tension now between the two. Perhaps they were collaborating to save face and planning away to wriggle out of helping me; no action was forthcoming to put an end to my legal struggle and save face of public perception.

There was a considerable build-up of sheer frustration on my part, and anger bubbling under the surface. Also, at the time, my Delica van had blown the heads. It too was trapped in time at the bottom of the infamous Toowoomba Range.

The mechanic had put the engine back together (so he said) and had it up and running. The day before I was to take the train and bus to collect the vehicle, the mechanic phoned to say the engine had failed the CO_2 test. It appeared the new parts that had been put on were faulty, leaving the only option to disassemble the motor and redo the repair. "Don't worry, that won't cost you," he assured me.

Six weeks later, the vehicle was still in bits and no fault could be plainly seen as to the cause of the mechanical breakdown. The new parts had tested okay under heat and pressure. The mechanic said, "In twenty years I've not come across anything like this. I am thinking now that the underlying problem could well be a hairline fracture in the top of the engine block. But I can't see any sign."

So, the jury was out, suspended in time by no clear knowing. Here I was, not blaming the mechanic because I knew he did not break it. He was there to fix it. I said, there being no coincidences, it was an extraordinary set of circumstances.

The extra financial pressure of costs associated with repair agitated my already heightened state of anxiety caused by the deafening sounds of silence, having had no replies nor expectation of a final, definitive outcome from my legal dilemma.

I was ready to explode but thought it better my van took the hit.

As fate had it, I was rescued from difficulty by an out-of-the-blue phone call offering me a contract for six months back in the laboratory of my previous school. It certainly took the pressure off financially and allowed me to gather patience to hold to my first view that my submissions were in the right hands and the process was underway, regardless of time delays.

With my car out of action since the day before Australia Day, 25 January 2012, and stranded at my son's home in Toowoomba, I made the decision to use the time to commence the draft of this sequel.

First, I grabbed a pen from the computer desk and a wad of blank A4 paper from the printer to draw up a thumbnail sketch of the outline of this book.

Monday, 26 January, I sat down to watch the evening news. To my surprise, there in the third bulletin was the senator, deputy leader of the opposition, shadow attorney-general, the Honourable Bill Gillard. He had taken umbrage at the tent embassy conundrum on Australia Day, and Bill had sprung to the press release to score some political points.

Senator Gillard was on his high horse, prattling about a "possible" security breach in regard to "the well-being" of the prime minister and the leader of the opposition, "the two most senior political leaders of the nation," Gillard stated.

I thought, *Isn't that bloody interesting?* Here was the senator, willing to publicly, at the drop of a hat, speculate and make issue of something that was less than a storm in a teacup, and yet, for nigh on five months, Bill Gillard had sat on my submission that, I contend, was explosive.

The senator too had written to the commissioner of the Australia Federal Police, seeking further investigation into the Australia Day tent embassy matter.

Eventually, the senator must act on my case submission. Which way he jumped was for his own conscience.

I saw for several months Bill Gillard had been unable to get the monkey off his back and rid himself of what was now a personal time bomb for him. My what-ifs suggested that the Hon. Senator Gillard and the minister, Vladimir Rossi, were working on a plan to ditch me.

It was around this time that my book *Without Prejudice* was first published. My aunt Evelyn had approached two other MPs, one of whom had spoken personally to my local MP, Vladimir Rossi. Her MP was also to pass on a copy of my book.

So, the senator and MP now knew that other parties within the federal parliament and the government were aware of my submission, and any dumping of me must at least look diplomatic and constitutional.

My anger and disappointment with the legal system and its cronies persisted. I was searching for an avenue I could prompt Senator Bill Gillard into action with.

My first fear was, as I said, not to piss Bill off. However, his non-action and zero communication were without doubt pissing me off.

Who did Gillard think he was?

Why should one man have absolute say in my destiny?

Had Gillard heard of the Magna Carta?

The Great Charter of English liberty was granted nearly eight hundred years ago on 15 June 1215. The Magna Carta was enacted to negate the autonomous rule of a tyrant, be it king, statesman, or clergyman; add to that list, in 2008, senators and ministers of the Australia Parliament.

The Magna Carta is the cornerstone of natural justice. It invokes an individual's right to be heard on a fair and level playing field. Even the village idiot has this basic right.

With all this nothingness and suspension in time, I searched for a strategy, an action to prompt the minister and senator to engage in talks, at the very least.

The most compelling necessity for me was to face my fears, confront the senator, and remind him by a registered letter, with a carbon copy to the minister, of the senator's pledge in his inaugural speech to parliament. I confronted Senator Bill Gillard with clauses 38, 39, and 40 of the Magna Carta, which pertain to natural justice of an individual.

Clause 38 of the Magna Carta states:

> No bailiff, on his own simple assertion, shall hence forth anyone to his law, without producing faithful witness in evidence.

Clause 39 of the Magna Carta states:

> No freeman shall be taken or imprisoned, or disseized, or outlawed, or exiled, or in any way harmed - - nor will we go upon him or send upon him - - save by the lawful judgement of his peers or by the law of the land.

Clause 40 of the Magna Carta states:

> To none will we sell, to none deny or delay, right or justice.

It is axiomatic that the conventions of these rules had been ignored by Gillard.

By sitting on my application to the federal executive, the senator had taken upon himself an autonomous stance, holding judgement of "his own simple assertion."

I had been incarcerated by his very non-specific performance. To me it was psychological warfare to have me strung out, suspended in time.

Clause 40 of the Magna Carta underlines and highlights the lack of consideration afforded to me as a constituent of the Commonwealth.

> To none will we sell, to none deny or delay, right or justice.

I contended that the Crime and Misconduct Commission were culpable, together with the Queensland Legal Services Commission, of failing to act, thus denying and delaying my right to justice.

I had a letter from the CMC stating that under their watchful eye, the QLSC were to deal with my complaint matter.

Three years on, no one would hand down a decision, since I had had my day in the kangaroo court.

The CMC having wiped the blood from their hands related to me, the complaint was then investigated by the commissioner. This commissioner was Bob Jenkins, the person I had officially complained about originally.

In Jenkins's reply, he affirmed he would never reply to any telephone call nor email nor written letter and closed my file. The CMC, being aware of this, had not challenged the commissioner's errant stance. Three years later, things were in abeyance, suspended in time, as everyone hoped I would go away.

Not so. I was now prepared to go to war and have resolution. Speed and surprise were known as the army's biggest weapons. Whatever outcome eventuated, after twenty or so years, it would be a pyrrhic victory. I knew I had run the race of my life, even won the race. I had knocked myself out, literally, but there had been no first-prize blue ribbon.

As many may be aware—and it is particularly pertinent to those anointed ones—even if you win the rat race, you're still a rat.

Nevertheless, resolution to my legal saga was my intention. What goes around comes around. I was still somewhat confident that the senator may champion my cause, without the need for a personal confrontation to force him to respond with a knee-jerk reaction like that of the Queensland Legal Services Commission.

Be under no miscomprehension: I am dishevelled, a direct product of my overwhelming tussle with individuals of the Queensland legal system, who have for twenty-two years ignored my hue and cry and allowed a felon to escape.

The individuals within the system have chosen to turn their backs and walk away from making a decision. They are no more than holding up the law of the jungle: dog eat dog, scrapping over the same bone, money.

It was greed, the pursuit of power, and an extreme lack of imagination, combined with lack of insight that perpetuated the madness of my world, allowing this twenty-two-year fracas to consume my life. I had simply not been able nor had opportunity to move on.

There was pent-up anger that would surely see my threat of exposing all payers implemented in my fall from grace. My intent was for them to be exposed and humiliated. I could no longer contain my disdain for the corrupt individuals of the legal and political system—namely, everyone who had sat on their hands, granted the authority to act yet had not the gumption. I intended to name those who had callously set upon me with no regard for the law, only in pursuit of their egotistical goal: to enhance their own financial ends. The action to name and shame had to cease, however. I desisted because of the libel laws.

I shall leave retribution to Christ, my Lord and Saviour. Naming of all parties to have them publicly shamed and made accountable for their criminal actions is not a viable course of action. These men and women of high community standing erroneously believe that they themselves are above the law. Not so. There is only one authority upon earth who oversees justice for all.

I expressly warned the minister, Vladimir Rossi, in my email to him on 27 February 2012, that I shall push on. After twenty-two years,

I did not see that they could not grasp my inexorable intent nor my obdurate stance.

Now the Minister Rossi and Senator Bill Gillard were in the loop, accountable for their own non-action.

It was never my intention to stitch anyone up. Everybody has free will. Karma is the product of decisions made. Taking responsibility for choices made is processing that karma. Denial and excuse are avoidance of responsibility. Karma hovers until it is dealt with. However, these people accepted public life and were in the position to keep law and order, in accordance with their legislation and written rules.

I submitted my first two manuscripts to a publisher for publication. However, both were rejected on the first round. My revenge, to name and shame individuals, was curtailed by professional advice. With that, I reverted to substituting actual dates, names, and places with contrived replacements, in order that people's privacy is maintained.

There are neither accidents nor coincidences. We reap what we sow. If you rob someone, you or a family member will be robbed in return. It is inescapable. What goes around comes around. Beware and be aware.

Christ Jesus said, "I am the Prince of Peace. However, I do not bring peace, but I bring a sword. For vengeance is mine. Everything is possible for him who believes" (Mark 9:23).

The sword is a double-edged blade, that which cuts through the veil and will force the truth. Two anagrams of *veil* are *evil* and *live*.

Most basically, all have the choice of either/or, evil or live, in relation to taking responsibility for decisions made and actions taken. This is karma.

What goes around comes back around to bite you on the bum or ensconce you in fecundity. Again, there is free will with regard to choosing, but you are impelled to make the right choice in alignment with the commandments chiselled in stone.

It has been duly noted that the Ten Commandments are not a multiple-choice question.

Not everybody is going to buy the advertisement. We will always have those poor in spirit. Just don't give them your power to make decisions for you.

I say this because this was my undoing. I trusted the word of a person who held himself out to be a righteous man decorated with the title of "solicitor" and holding a "trust."

The only thing we get to keep in this our world is our word.

It is the "I" in your word that creates your world.

There are many wolves in sheep's clothing. Ruck and Rathdowney were wolves of the highest order, in my opinion, although I could name others who would be fierce competitors for the analogy and title.

Sean Ruck's true colours were seen as being the hidden enemy in the woodpile when he rang into the district court on Friday, 15 March 2009, to scuttle my chances of success. I was still beleaguered as to the capricious savagery of Ruck toward me, his paying client. I can only imagine there was a financial sweetener from Rathdowney in it for him.

But greed would see Ruck try to take another bite out of me for $5,000, for which he threatened to sue me after the initial hearing. My remark was, "Clown." To me, "clown" is a mild expression for a bullying thug with no conscience—a callous, cruel, gruff individual, assigned to the devil's work.

My retort to Sean Ruck now would be, "Grow a heart or get back to the jungle, Crusty."

Simply grotesque. To add another colourful phrase, allegedly used but denied by Senator Gillard in describing statements of James Hector regarding the refugee children overboard saga in 2001: "a lying rodent."

Ah! The rats pop their heads up again. However, if we compare and contrast rats to solicitors and barristers, it can be seen that solicitors and barristers do things the rats won't.

While the rats do not have the capacity to reason, solicitors and barristers do, and being mere mortals, they are responsible for their choices, come hell or high water. Let the chips fall where they may. So be it.

The first time I was bitten by a rat was in the laboratory, mucking out the cage housing two female rats and a litter of eight pinkies. The mother sprang two feet from the corner of the cage and caught me by surprise, biting me on the thumb.

It was the first and only time I was bitten by a laboratory rat. After the many years of handling these critters, I was a little miffed that I had been bitten.

My summation of that only bite was that it was an animal instinct to protect its own. For me it was "Once bitten, twice shy," as the saying goes.

The second time I was bitten was when I was mucked around in the Queensland District Court. Again, those of the legal system were protecting their own. I didn't see that bite coming either.

The mother rat protecting her babies I can forgive. The administration and the legal system I hold in contempt for the treatment dished out to me over twenty-two years, and particularly on the day of the lower court in March 2009, I do not forgive!

It will never be okay to be maligned, falsely accused, chewed up, and spat out, wasted by the process of man's perceived justice, which is the illusion created with smoke and mirrors to manipulate a contrived outcome.

Out of seven billion people on our plane, it appears that I am the only one who insists that the justice dealt me by individuals of the Queensland legal system will *never* be okay!

The district court hearing, interfered with by Rathdowney and Ruck, was a sham, a kangaroo court by any reasonable person's reckoning.

Yet those I have challenged do not have red faces. I am ashamed for their blatant ignorance and avoidance of the truth: mature adults flouting the rules. These individuals, believing they're above the law, are white knuckled, holding on to their lies and perceived power.

They are defensive, using any foul trick they can muster to cover their tracks and bury the truth. The power of the political and legal system, I contend, is that they can stymie the press and media releases, making it a one-way flow of their perceived, manipulated truth.

My book, *Without Prejudice,* was written as a direct result of my frustration with being blocked from airing my side of the story. The book, published in the United States, has recently been released. I intend to send all those I consider "involved" promotional literature to raise their awareness of their meddling. There has been no lawful resolution to this saga in which they have been involved, only delay after delay after delay, for twenty-two years.

Whenever was black, white or white, black?

Those involved may well try to avoid re-evaluation, but they all have had opportunity to come clean. This forced truth is the energy that will shed light on the flawed system and has the thrust to turn the wheel of what goes around comes around.

The wheel of fortune turns. Everybody has a cross to bear by the rudimentary rules of karma, like it or not.

As we all on earth are allegedly hurtled through space and time at a speed of approximately thirteen hundred kilometres per hour and rotate once every twenty-four hours, this karma is played out on the flat earth plane. Existence is cyclic, a never-ending story, not linear and final.

That's the good news. Each, at the end of the day, collects his winnings or goes home broke. With exception of the immortals who do it forever, no one gets out of this life alive—not even the anointed ones.

The wheel turns. Life goes on, no one escaping the wheel of fortune.

An add-on to this train of thought is the pattern of history repeating itself.

On an individual level, we see patterns of recurring situations, be they good or indifferent.

Wayne Dwyer, a philosopher, coined a phrase regarding the habitual patterning in our lives: "You cannot get enough of what you don't want."

Life goes on regardless of awareness. The karmic wheel of fortune turns ever so slowly at times, but it turns; sometimes in retrograde, yet it turns and turns; no one can stop the wheel and what is destined by the phenomenon of cause and effect.

The man of the twentieth century, Albert Einstein, made comment back in 1929 which I believe alludes to the phenomenon of cause and effect. Einstein said, "Everything is determined … by forces over which we have no control. It is determined for the insect as well as for the star, Human beings, vegetables, or cosmic dust—we all dance to a mysterious tune, intoned in the distance by an invisible piper."

In 1930, Einstein was quoted as saying, "I am the artist's model." One such drawing that captured my interest was a black-and-white sketch by Lutta Waloscek from 1995. There exist many photographs and sketches of Albert, depicting him as the "nutty professor," a tribute too and a term of endearment for this remarkable man.

CHAPTER 2

The Wheel of Fortune

The wheel of fortune is a euphemism for karma. Karma can be summed up as that which goes around comes around. Similarly, the wheel of fortune is the dynamic of yin and yang, God's fundamental rule of cause and effect.

There are no secrets, only those perceived to be by man's thinking. Every deed by man in time, in time is revealed. Not one sparrow drops to the ground without being acknowledged as part of creation by God, himself/herself.

Regions of the earth plane, nations, countries, colonies, states, territories, towns, and villages all exude their own karma. It comes from the understanding of the saying "Birds of a feather flock together."

It is why the anointed ones, as I have labelled the individuals of the legal and political systems, are like-minded. They share the same beliefs and tend to emanate similar traits of character. The majority have studied law at university; they have all been groomed and conditioned to think similarly. The anointed ones act, too, so very predictably. Hence my formed opinion and my exclamation, "Fools! *Same same but different.*"

Therefore, they band together: to protect their species. Yet they are dysfunctional as a group because individuals within their group seek more and more power to dominate, accruing prestige to rule their communities, not just in the legal system. Within the system itself, is a power struggle, and what eventuates is a peck order. Very much like a caste structure or class order within a society or a cult, and not too dissimilar to Fred Flintstone's Buffalo Club.

I put the question, "Who would don a black robe and a white camelhair wig, take up a wooden gavel with an anvil, and preside over laws of the land?" Then, for what reason?

To me, Jan Ernest Gainsworthy, it is surely a glorified front for a cult, controlling and suppressing the free will of man in our society, playing God without a conscience.

The law and politics are intertwined and are so important in our world that every individual should be involved. The people have the power. Definitely, the structure of community should not be left solely to solicitors, barristers, and politicians to steer the future course of a free society.

My bitter experience has found the cult wanting. The cult adorns itself in black robes and white camelhair wigs, to administer a legal system. Yet, this cult fails the masses concerning a transparent justice system. There are some who put themselves above the law. The only difference between God and the solicitors, barristers, and judges is that God does not think or label himself/herself, any of those!

I have admonished for years, "Don't follow the cobblestone path of the Roman model, for the Roman civilization crumbled like the walls of Jericho."

While most within the cult may be hold fast to moral objectives, it is also well known that the road to hell is paved with good intentions. Having good intentions, when there follows no action, is just empty, contrived words or silence. It is like a pie-in-the-sky promise: hot air with nothing of substance.

The Roman model of controlling the populace was so-called "bread and circus." The Romans' hidden agenda was to keep the masses fed with bread and entertained with a circus; these were measures for controlling the unaware crowd. The Romans built the Colosseum and entertained their citizens with barbaric acts of human cruelty, with stoushes between warring gladiators. Christians were thrown to the lions. It was simply outrageous and iniquitous, yet all was sanctioned by the 'powers that be' in those times. And, karma did follow!

Today we emulate the same bread-and-circus model as the Romans.

The Queensland state government built a modern-day colosseum at Robina, Gold Coast. They named it Skilled Park, the home of the Titans. The stadium, plastered with the Queensland government logo, was built in an area between a high school, the new Gold Coast Hospital, the Robina railway station, and one of the largest shopping centres in the southern hemisphere. The region is densely populated with residential town-house communities and commercial offices, with no purpose-built car park for football patrons. There is no car park accessible to cater for the crowd rolling up to the stadium on game day. (Naming rights have been *sold*; it is now, in 2014, the Cbus Super Stadium. However, the Queensland logo persists on the western outer wall. Cbus is an industry superannuation fund company.)

Every game day and event at the stadium causes horrendous traffic congestion. The police are paid from the public purse to block off roads and streets, and are required to enforce the no-parking restrictions in the area and to allow the residences access only.

The general public are required to catch public transport or park their cars in zones and be shuttled by buses to the ground from five kilometres away. The scene is bedlam, an invariable circus. Add to this, the visiting team's supporters, such as the Bulldogs or Saint George.

Supporters en masse form a sea of amusement-seekers wandering around from the fenced construction site of the Titans' Centre of Excellence building to the stadium before kick-off, then back from the stadium through the same construction maze after the final siren.

The bread is a costly offering: ten dollars for a pie and chips, and seven dollars for a plastic 425 millilitre cup of mid-strength beer.

I was given the opportunity to go to a Titans match on a couple of occasions as a club member when a friend of a friend was unable to attend.

I accompanied my long-standing mate RJ Morton to the ground. Morton is an avid National Rugby League follower and a founding member of the Gold Coast Titans.

RJ and I drove from Tweed Heads to the car park facility, having then to go through the process of parking the car, waiting for a bus, shuttling to the bus/train terminal, and then walking the final 500 metres to the stadium.

Being at the stadium early, we stopped at the members' bar for a couple of schooners of Victoria bitter, poured from beer taps on chilled fonts into glasses.

Two weeks later, a similar occasion arose again, and Morton and I proceeded to the members' bar. I ordered two Victoria bitter schooners of beer. I was informed by the bar steward that they no longer served heavy beer on tap in glasses.

"What's this?" I asked. "Why not? Just a fortnight ago you were serving heavy beer on tap."

"The government has put new rules in place. There are no longer heavy beers on tap, and we are no longer allowed to serve patrons with glass due to of the recent spate of 'glassings' in pubs on the Gold Coast."

I was astounded. "It's a further restriction of civil liberty. We are in the members' bar of a football club, not the swill of some blood house," I replied.

"You can have a heavy out of a stubby if you prefer," said the steward.

"Okay, give me two stubbies of VB. I certainly don't want a mid-strength beer poured into a plastic cup," said I.

With that the bar steward took two stubbies of Victoria bitter from the fridge, removed their twist-tops, and, to my absolute horror, proceeded to pour them into plastic receptacles. "You're kidding," I said.

"They're the new rules," replied the steward.

Weeks later, another friend won four free tickets to a Titans football game from a radio quiz. I was given two of them.

I phoned my old chum Rick, who is an avid sports follower, and related that I had one spare ticket. "Would you like to go?" It was a Friday night game, and we arranged to meet up outside the ticket office at the stadium.

Rick had taken a crowded free bus to the stadium and was indignant about the cattle-prodding and disarray of the experience just to get to the game. He was aghast at the automated beer dispensing and the presentation of flat beer in a plastic cup.

Rick is the only person I know who shares my sentiment that the whole set-up is a government-controlled restriction of people's free choice. So much so that they indicate to the crowd when to cheer and promote booing as the visiting team runs onto the paddock

Rick is a two-packet-a-day cigarette smoker and was riled by the total ban on smoking within Able Park, since it is a government facility.

Rick was required to get a pass out from the ground through a security checkpoint to a non-restricted smoking area, in which no alcoholic drinks were allowed. Rick refused point-blank to play that game and went to the gents to smoke his cigarettes. "It's outrageous," he said. "I feel like a little schoolboy sneaking a cigarette." At our parting after game's end, Rick said, "Thanks for the ticket, and I've enjoyed your company, but I will never come to this stadium again. I feel like a second-class citizen with no individual rights. What's happening to society? How does the rest of the crowd put up with this bullshit? I mean it. I will never set foot in this place again!"

By the dwindled attendance reported in a recent newspaper article, one could surmise there are other football followers who hold the same view as Rick and are staying away from Cbus Super Stadium.

The idealist Centre of Excellence building is now considered a white elephant. It has been fraught with legal battles with the builder and added costs of construction and furnishings. As of the end of 2014, the building is still unfinished and has not met requirements to be fully certified for occupation, which is the reason why the Titans' property arm cannot obtain full tenancy for the building.

Startling revelations from a newspaper article tell us that a judge of the federal court in Brisbane on Friday, 23 March 2012, found that the Gold Coast Titans (property) Pty Ltd were, "prima facie," insolvent in relation to the Centre of Excellence building, and the football arm of the club was liable for the $13 million-dollar debt. This, added to the club's existing debt, escalates their total indebtedness to $35 million dollars.

Speculation is that if the Titans are in the hole for $35 million, then they may well not be able to climb out. The Gold Coast NRL football club may fold.

The club is on the wheel of fortune: what goes around comes around. History shows the folding of three other Gold Coast rugby clubs due to financial pressures and an inadequate supporter base. The clubs that went under were the Sea Gulls, the Crushers, and the Gold Coast Charges.

The Queensland state government will have Skills Park Stadium as a white elephant on their hands if the Titans football arm goes under. It is a daunting possibility, and Gold Coast residents will have lost another locally based rugby football team.

Another glaring illustration of the ebb and flow, like a pendulum swinging, is the result of the Queensland state election on 27 March 2012.

Labor came in on a landslide vote in December 1989 and went out on a landslide protest vote. With that said, how is Neville Chamberlin's new cabinet going to perform?

The coalition has been such an ineffective opposition for all those years. What has changed? Nothing! Except the perceived image of Neville Chamberlin. The wheel turns, and if history repeats itself, then it will be a short-lived government.

Neville Chamberlin simply won't do for the State of Queensland. Already, in a penny-pinching exercise, his government has axed the Queensland Premier's Literacy Awards set up by Petro Beer in 1998, their purpose being to build a "creative culture" within Queensland.

One political commentator called it a "punitive" measure to save the taxpayers $244,000, but at what cost to developing literacy? The question was also put: "what sort of government would make that such a priority in the first week of their elected term?"

We shall wait and see. Some political commentators may see the crushing defeat as a protest vote, a backlash in relation to the federal government and Jillian Gardner's "ides of March" against the prime minister R. Kramer, at the time.

The wheel is always turning. Julius Caesar was reportedly a dictator and statesman. He was knifed in the back twenty-three times in the Roman senate in the year 44 BC. That is 2,056 years ago, and nothing has seemingly changed.

"The more things change; the more things stay the same" is an old adage.

So, was Bronwyn Anderson playing the part of Caesar and the voting public that of Brutus?

Anderson, unlike Kramer, was warned of events. However, we have the benefit of written history and the 20/20 vision of hindsight.

Every past event can be scrutinized and re-evaluated upon light being shone by the revolutions of the karmic wheel of fortune.

"Beware the ides of March."

I recently read on Wikipedia another account of Caesar's demise that suggested that Brutus and his assailants did not lie in wait for Caesar, but another individual protesting at unfair treatment; he was waving a knife around and there was a skirmish. Caesar, unarmed, turned away and tripped, leaving him face down to suffer twenty-three stabs to his back. Only the second wounding was fatal, according to the report. When they rolled Caesar face up, the person he first saw was Brutus. Caesar's final words were, "Oh no, not you too, Brutus."

Julius Caesar was appointed by the Roman Republic as an *extraordinary magistrate*.

The office of dictator was a legal innovation of the Roman Senate and only appointed so long as the Romans were at war in Italy. The office of dictator had absolute authority over ordinary magistrates. Hence, Caesar was not a dictator as such, but merely held the title and carried out his duties according to the rules.

There was no seemingly justifiable reason for Brutus to lie in wait with assailants, as the story has gone.

Caesar was taken hostage for ransom by four individuals years prior to being appointed to the Senate. The ransom money was paid by the Roman Senate and Caesar set free. While in the custody of the extortionists, Caesar warned them he would hunt them down and kill them. They believed at the time Caesar was making idle threats; he had neither the authority nor the capability to follow through.

Years later, it so happened that Caesar tracked down and captured the four kidnappers. He took them back to Rome for punishment. The Wikipedia article suggested Caesar showed some human compassion when dealing with these four chaps. Caesar was lenient with them and merely had their throats cut, as opposed to having all four shamefully drawn and quartered. Such were the times.

"The good old days" have now a unique perspective.

"History repeats itself" is a frequently quoted saying. Perhaps a function of karma?

Essentially, the pondering of 'history repeats itself' is food for thought, which is also known as 'grist for the mill.'

As a bizarre example of history repeating itself, I shall allude to two historical events that I believe are linked to and illustrate the notion that indeed history does repeat itself. My examples are the Hindenburg disaster in 1936 and the Space Shuttle Challenger disaster in 1986.

The similarities between these disasters are amazing to me. Firstly, the Hindenburg was attempting to dock with its mooring mast. The airship docking was being telecast live by a newsreel coverage when the explosion, followed by incineration, occurred.

The newsreel commentator became emotional and, ultimately, speechless.

The Space Shuttle Challenger too, was being telecast live by CNN on 28 January 1986, and exploded seventy-three seconds after lift-off. The CNN commentators were speechless. No one was quite sure what had happened.

Both the Hindenburg and Challenger's explosions were the result of free hydrogen gas being ignited.

There was also much controversy over the causes of both disasters.

The Hindenburg was three hundred feet in the air when it exploded at the US Navy base in New Jersey in 1936. At the time, the United States had a military embargo on helium, and the Germans were forced to use hydrogen in its Zeppelins. The Germans believed they had a good safety record in relation to using hydrogen to float their craft.

The situation in Germany in 1921, would indicated otherwise. What eventuated was, an airship exploded due to free hydrogen in its hanger and subsequently took out another four Zeppelins in neighbouring hangers, wiping out the entire fleet of five. According to my reckoning, that is not a sound safety record.

This incident occurred fifteen years prior to the Hindenburg disaster, which ended travel by hydrogen-filled airships forever. Perhaps, with 20/20 hindsight, the loss of five airships in 1921, due to free hydrogen exploding, may well have been deemed then, to be too greater risk for passenger travel.

A report retrieved from Wikipedia details what the Zeppelin historian Dr Douglas Robinson pointed out in his 1964 book, *LZ-129 Hindenburg*.

Dr Robinson stated, "Although ignition of free hydrogen by static discharge had become a favoured hypothesis, no such discharge was seen by any of the witnesses who testified at the official investigation into the accident back in 1937."

Dr Robinson further stated,

> Nevertheless, within the past year, I have located an observer, Professor Mark Heald of Princeton, New Jersey, who undoubtedly saw St Elmo's fire flickering

along the airships back, a good minute before the fire broke out. Standing outside the main gate to the Naval Air Station, he watched, together with his wife and son, as the Zeppelin approached the mast and dropped her bow-lines. A minute later by Mr Heald's estimation, he first noticed a dim "blue flame" flickering along the backbone girder about one-quarter the length abaft the bow to the tail. There was time for him to remark to his wife, "Oh, heavens, the thing is afire," for her to reply, "Where?" and for him to answer, "Up along the top ridge" – before there was a big burst of flaming hydrogen from a point he estimated to be about one-third the ship's length from the stern.

The Wikipedia commentator adds,

Unlike other witnesses to the fire whose view to the port side of the ship had the light of the setting sun behind the ship, Professor Heald's view of the starboard side of the ship against the backdrop of the darkening evening sky would have made the dim blue light of static discharge on the top of the ship more easily visible.

Another theory, dismissed, is that the disaster was caused by the sabotage of the Third Reich.

Yet another theory, is that a passenger suicided by firing a gun. Interestingly, a Luger was said to have been found among the wreckage. The report also claimed that the Luger had one chamber fired. My invitation is for you to be the judge.

I am satisfied the faint blue flame flickering along the Zeppelin's backbone was St Elmo's fire, a static discharge of electrical energy that would ignite free hydrogen.

The Zeppelin would have been statically charged from the air polishing the outer skin of the ship while in transit. Once earthed, it would be like the discharge of a thundercloud that produces the phenomenon of lightning.

In nearly every school's physics laboratory is a piece of apparatus called a Van De Graff generator. This equipment is designed to generate static electricity. Electrons are wiped off a circulating rubber belt and collected at the top of a large metal dome.

When conditions are ripe, 7,000–10,000 volts can be stored and discharged using an earthing sphere. The static charge can leap seven centimetres to discharge.

In demonstrations to classes of students, it is arranged for the Van De Graff to be discharged and switched off. The teacher selects a student, usually female because of her long straight, fine hair, and has the student stand on a wooden crate to isolate her from being grounded.

Before the apparatus is switched on, the student rests one (or both) hand on the metal dome of the machine; the Van De Graff is then started.

On a fine day with low humidity, the student's body will become charged, and the hair on her head will rise and stick out due to like charges repelling each other. It's a sight.

Another demonstration I have only seen twice is by in the same manner charging the pupil with static electricity. The discharge is directed to the barrel of an activated Bunsen burner. In a blue flash as the student earths, the gas ignites, lighting the Bunsen. Spectacular!

Challenger had theorists proposing it was not combustion of fuels that caused the disaster seventy-three seconds after blast-off from the Kennedy Space Center in Florida. At the time, theorists argued that it was the rapid deceleration and not combustion fuels. Since it is widely accepted that the cause of the disaster was that the O-rings of the solid fuel booster tanks were compromised by temperature, and the cold shrank the O-rings, allowing hydrogen to escape and ultimately ignite, blasting the shuttle into pieces.

The hydrogen explosion did not kill the astronauts instantly. The command module where the astronauts were housed was blown clear and intact, eight kilometres above the earth's surface. The seven would have survived the explosion and been alive while the capsule reached terminal velocity, killing them on impact with the surface of the Atlantic Ocean.

Both disasters, the Hindenburg and the Challenger, were the result of free hydrogen exploding.

Hydrogen is the most abundant element in the universe. It is the smallest and lightest of all elements. Hence its use in airships: hydrogen allows airships to float because hydrogen is lighter than air.

Chemists consider hydrogen a metal because of the way it reacts with non-metals such as oxygen.

Helium, the second-smallest and second-lightest element, is a noble gas. The molecular structure of helium has a full outer shell of electrons, which makes it very unreactive—inert. Helium is a non-volatile gas, and it is not flammable like hydrogen.

The United States, because it was not involved in war with Germany in 1936, placed a military embargo on helium. I do not understand why the USA would ban helium under the circumstances.

If the Germans had helium available, then why ban helium and force the Germans to use hydrogen, with such disastrous outcomes? And why did the Germans bow to the pressure?

Science shows us that the Hindenburg disaster may well have been avoided if the Germans had used helium.

To demonstrate the explosiveness of free hydrogen gas, there is a conventional laboratory experiment, called the pop test. Three centimetres of magnesium are placed in a test tube to react with 5–10 millilitres of two-molar hydrochloric acid, the reaction generating heat, hydrogen gas, a salt, and water.

With another test tube inverted over the first, containing magnesium and spirits of salt, the hydrogen gas is collect in the inverted tube. As long as the second test tube is kept bottom up, the hydrogen will not escape because it is lighter than air.

A lighted tapper is put to the mouth of the inverted test tube, and a pronounced *pop* can be heard. This is a positive test for the presence of free hydrogen.

I attended a laboratory technicians' professional development day on the campus of Griffith University, Gold Coast, back in 2007. It was a chance to catch up with people of the profession and some old work buddies.

Distracted by the moment and enjoying a couple of lunchtime beers at the bar, Jacinta and I overshot the lunch hour by fifteen minutes. We arrived back to the afternoon session those minutes behind, conspicuously late and unable to slip in the back unnoticed as planned.

The entry was at the front of the conference room, where two postgraduate students from the Griffith University science faculty were giving a demonstration on, of all things, hydrogen. I apologised for our lateness and gestured to move to the back of the room. One of the young demonstrators said, "As you are standing up the front, you can be our audience volunteer."

I thought it a small price to pay for my little indiscretion, and besides I had done this stuff many times before. I replied a little coyly, "Only too pleased to assist."

First, they generated hydrogen in a half-litre conical flask, with hydrochloric acid and magnesium added. The flask was sealed with a one-holed rubber bung, with a tube for the gas and pressure to escape. The end of the tube was placed into a glass trough of detergent and water. The hydrogen bubbling through the liquid produced a large cluster of hydrogen-filled bubbles.

I was asked to scoop up some bubbles, wearing protective gloves, and then to hold my hand out for the demonstrator to ignite the bubbles with a lit taper. There was a series of little *pop*s from the hydrogen exploding. I thought that was a very impressive demonstration of surface area ratios and noted it for future reference.

I gestured to move to my seat to sit down. However, a demonstrator said, "Please, we have one more task for you, Jan. We need your assistance to hold this metre-long dowel outstretched while we put a lighted taper to the balloon taped to the other end."

"Surely," I said. I had filled balloons before with hydrogen, and I had demonstrated the ignition of hydrogen in a balloon similarly.

The postgraduate students had filled a balloon with hydrogen prior to the session and had mounted it on the dowel handle. The balloon was about 25–30 centimetres across, so there was a fair volume of hydrogen gas contained inside. I extended my arm and held the balloon just above head height; the demonstrator with his lighted taper, also mounted on dowel, ignited the balloon.

Well, *ka-boom*! Up went the tiles of the suspended ceiling. Everyone was aghast. It was a jaw-dropper. No one expected such a startling explosion.

People from neighbouring buildings ran out to see what had happened. I postulate the postgraduate students had not anticipated such an explosion either. I asked one of them, "What was that? I have done similar demonstrations, but never with anywhere near that reaction."

Their reply was, "Oh, we put oxygen in with the hydrogen."

"Damn," I said. "You buggers, I think you certainly got all of us with that."

The formula for the chemical reaction is this:

$$2 H_2 + O_2 + \text{ignition/heat} = 2 H_2O$$

This reaction can be reversed by disassociation of hydrogen and oxygen by the process of electrolysis. Interestingly, for every one molecule of oxygen, we generate two molecules of hydrogen.

For the imagination, hydrogen and oxygen may be hypothesised as the elements responsible for the Big Bang. The Big Bang may have been the reaction of hydrogen and oxygen and heat to give water, H_2O. Now, joining the dots. The biologists say we, as humans, are made up of between 78 per cent and 87 per cent water. Could we go that far back to the Big Bang?

A most widely speculated claim of history repeating itself is that of the similarities between the assassinations of Abraham Lincoln and John Fitzgerald Kennedy. These presidents of the United States were elected to office 100 years apart: Lincoln in 1860 and JFK in 1960. Both were civil rights activists. Both Lincoln and Kennedy were shot in the back of the head on a Friday, with their wives present. Their assassins were both known by three names, comprising fifteen letters; John Wilkes Booth and Lee Harvey Oswald. Both assassins were killed before being brought to trial.

Further coincidences include that Lincoln's successor had the surname Johnson—Andrew, born in 1808—while JFK's successor was Lyndon Johnson, born in 1908. For the sceptics, "You be the judge."

Since writing this passage, over five years ago, I have been shown footage of the assignation of JFK, and it appears the chauffer turned and shot the President at point-blank range. Again, you be the judge.

With the benefit of twenty-twenty hindsight, we as a global community have opportunity to learn from the past. Many say the past is the past and cannot be changed.

Some, such as Joe Noel Rathdowney, have attempted to bury their pasts. Karma is the consequence of an individual's choices. Rathdowney made a choice. He is held by the unseen forces to be responsible for the choice he made affecting my life twenty-two years ago.

Sean Jeffrey Ruck will reap his karma too, for the choices and actions he has made without conscientious thought about people's lives. Ruck, with Jerry Abbott of counsel, buried evidence in the Black Rock,

Queensland, Supreme Court files. They were able to stave off an appeal from an innocent party, using their positions, power, and knowledge of how the system can be manipulated.

The case was heard in chambers in the presence of the judge and legal teams only; the plaintiff and the defendants were excluded. His Honour Justice Baden-Clay ruled for the plaintiff, on the blind acceptance of a hand-scribbled, contrived order of counsel, Jerry Abbott, on an A4 sheet of paper with Ruck's law firm's letterhead. Behind closed doors, the unquestioned verdict was manipulated far, Without Prejudice.

Sadly, for now they have got away with it. There are undoubtedly many more buried truths. It is certainly too late for one of the innocent parties, who has passed from cancer.

I did not invent being ripped off. Fraud has been going on for eons. But I am beleaguered: Within the Queensland justice system, not one person has adopted nor sides with my plight. No one has been willing to help me attain justice, as is written by their rules.

I have on many occasions asked myself, "How can one in office not have the conscience simply to do the right thing?"

The right thing would be a refreshing change! Indeed, to change the legal system's dogged stance and perception would be to restore one's faith in the system. Perhaps they could allow the truth to shed light on a flawed system, but that would take courage and compassion—conviction of what is fundamentally right and fair for all.

Seeing through the eye of the heart is the truth proffered by the Native Americans. The heart does not think like the head but knows unmistakably what truth is. From any perspective, the truth does not change. It may be hammered and kinked out of shape, yet it is malleable, like a copper sheet.

The buried truth has been exhumed. Light has been shed on the trail of deceit, and surely karma will follow as recriminations to those having to deal with the consequences of their choices made by the ignorance.

That is my truth.

For the anointed ones, it is an affront, easily denied by those without conscience. They know that their buried secrets will stay buried because complacency is entrenched in today's society. With complacency comes the attitude, "Who cares?"

I suggest you care about the world and the community you live in, together with caring about the consequences of your actions and non-actions.

Buddha advocated taking the middle road, to avoid the poles of extremes and seek the peace that is in the centre. Shirley MacLaine, in her book *Out on a Limb*, encourages everyone to take the inward journey because that is where real calm and peace are attained. Yet one must go out on a limb, take a calculated risk, as that is where the sweetest fruit is to be found.

On that middle road, don't forget to stop and smell the flowers. Rest awhile between the ephemeral stepping stones of life.

Withdraw from the worldly din at regular periods. Cease all work and centre your true being by adopting Shirley MacLaine's inward journey to peace. Forgive. Be kind to yourself.

Nature's elixir for optimum health is the combination of fresh air, clean drinking water, and sunshine, together with a healthy diet, exercise, balance of work and play, all bound with the "attitude of gratitude."

Also, laugh out loudly. All is well.

CHAPTER 3

Recriminations: A Different Perspective

The long-enforced waiting for a determination from Senator Gillard allowed me the time to think, "What if?" What if the Tobjoano deal had come off twenty-two years ago? Joe Rathdowney would probably be a close business associate; I may be still married and living in the lap of luxury.

I could be a corporate director turning over millions a year, ignorant of the unjust processes of the legal system and the one authority on earth. I could be promoting the splendour of accumulating assets and amulets. I could be dripping with gold chains to show off my successes, in contention for being the richest man in the cemetery.

But would I be happy having missed twenty-two years of overwhelming struggle, which has shaped my present-day character and knowing?

Answer: in my darkest hours, at my lowest points, I would have danced with Nimrod himself to have the burden of injustice lifted from me.

However, like fraud, injustice was not my invention either. Both fraud and injustice have been reportedly going on for millennia. This is another sticking point—the fact that nearly everybody I speak to, and no doubt you the reader, has experienced, at some point, injustice.

"Good luck with justice" is the echoing, continuous sound reverberating from the masses.

The sound must be coming from the rear ends of the ostriches. Even those in authority and with authority have, in relation to my case, had their heads in the sand. I can only surmise that, after all the injustice dealt me and which has flowed as water under the bridge, the legal fraternity has falsely hoped that one day I will hit the wall, forget the ordeal, and give up.

Experts and academics in the fields of law and social order have tabled volumes documenting inadequacies and anomalies of our legal system, yet no one has made it a political platform for reform. Surely, we as an intelligent society cannot stand by knowingly and allow these injustices to be perpetuated unchecked, for future generations to unravel, simply because we are too complacent to bother about a dysfunctional legal system.

Who cares? This question seems to be the art of complacency, along with, "It's not my problem." Charles Dickens was quoted by Murray Dunn, a journalist of the *Sun-Herald*: "The one great principle of the English law is to make business for itself."

This remark of Dickens's illustrates that he too was aware that the legal system feeds itself first, with regard to neither justice nor accountability to serve the people.

Murray Dunn's feature article in the "Law & Order: The Courts" segment of the *Sun-Herald* on Sunday, 29 May 2009 is referenced below to highlight the fact that academics and experts in the field of law know unshakably that our system is dysfunctional and failing our democratic society.

The feature article was dedicated to Willie Evans's latest book, *Our Corrupt Legal System: Why Everyone Is a Victim (Except Rich Criminals)*. The article was headed "Land where the criminals roam free."

The Australia legal system is a cabal run in the interests of lawyers.

According to Murray Dunn, Evans claims that about 95 per cent of people tried for crimes are guilty. Yet despite this, in Australia, 50 per cent of those arraigned are acquitted by our courts. In Europe, however, strikingly almost 100 per cent are convicted of the charge if tried.

Also, it is claimed that under the European system it was far less likely for an innocent party to be convicted erroneously.

The final point Evans makes is that he believes there is no willingness to change the ineffective legal system because "our politics is dominated by one occupation – lawyers."

I concur. This is the most salient point as to why there has been no change for thousands of years. Barristers, solicitors, and politicians have perpetuated the misconception that they are public servants and they are here to help. Barristers, solicitors, judges, and politicians take the highbrow stance that they know what's best for us, the little people, and a little white lie is acceptable to free the guilty and jail the innocent.

Society has been conditioned to accept the anointed ones' rulings as final. I too held the perception that the legal system was just, until my bitter experience changed all that. The boat we are in is being driven by what has been done in the past. This model is a misperception of believing the wake is pushing the vessel. And, you little people, "Don't rock the boat."

This is one of Wayne Dwyer's analogies: People peering over the stern of the ship watching the churned waters of the propellers and the tracks of the past without bothering to look beyond the bow of the ship to make sure it's not headed for troubled waters. There is seemingly no one steering the ship, or worse, the ship has no rudder. Ask, "Who is at the helm?" No one knows; they are all peering over the stern, focusing on the churned waters of the past.

This delinquent behaviour is akin to a person doing the same thing over and over with the expectation of a different outcome.

I would holler, "Stop! Get your bearings, good people. The ship's about to run aground."

The crew of the Queensland legal system administers such a tight ship. Their cloistered cult closed ranks on my claim to have investment funds returned to me, which I had deposited into a solicitor's trust account.

Prior to my submission to the federal executive of the Australian Parliament, I had written or emailed no fewer than fifty solicitors, canvassing for some legal support for my claim to have Rathdowney account. With the elucidation of vital new evidence, I sought advice in relation to the unconscionable actions of Sean Ruck.

My intended approach would certainly have been broadcast directly to Rathdowney and Ruck by a handful within the system that received my plea for assistance. I was surprised that as many as 20 per cent of the law firms I contacted replied to the canvassing. The covering letter and the letter that was titled, "Without Prejudice" is included below.

Jan Ernest Gainsworthy

Justice for my plight

July 2011

Lytton and Co.
Solicitors
Brisbane

Covering Letter

Dear Sirs

I am canvassing for a Law Firm / Solicitor accomplished in litigation and your company has stood-out.

The Law Firm I wish to engage must be willing to act for me in my claims against a practising Solicitor, who to this date has proved to be the Master of escape.

My expectation is that there will be no more, "long enforced waiting" for me, and the Law Firm will cause an expedient and successful completion of my case that has up until now caused overwhelming emotional exhaustion.

I have attached a letter to introduce myself and give an explanation of my position thus far.

Justice for All
Yours faithfully

Jan Ernest Gainsworthy

Jan Ernest Gainsworthy

Lytton & Co. LAW FIRM
P.O. Box 1305
George Street
Brisbane Qld 4103

Without Prejudice
Justice for my Plight

Dear Sirs

I have for twenty years sought real justice in order to have my funds that were deposited into a solicitor's Trust account, rightfully and legally returned to me.

I am in need of your help to force the Law firm of Rathdowney MacDraw to account for the moneys I deposited by bank cheques into their Trust account back in 1990. I still hold the two original receipts.

The same scheme, you, Lytton & Co, had dealings with as Solicitors for the Plaintiff. Up until now Rathdowney has been the Master of escape by saying Joana (Fletcher) was his client and Rathdowney acted on his client's instruction.

In 1990 I had just sold my Newsagency business in Tin Can Bay; the solicitor Ruck was my solicitor for the sale.

I was introduced to the Rathdowney, solicitor at law and Kevin Joana, Managing Director of C.K.F. Finance by my then brother-in-law. I was lead to believe at all times Rathdowney and Joana were business partners that had put together the Tobjoano Over Sea's Loans operation but now I can conclude they were partners. I have ASIC records in my possession that substantiates this.

The agreement was that I as an INVESTOR, <u>not a borrower</u>; and the returns on my deposited funds would be double and I would have in principle a pre-approved loan @ 10% for up to $500 K. The 100% returns were not because it was "high risk" but because of the time restraints on the C.K.F. Finance to complete the overseas loan transaction with the Banking Consortium now in Hong Kong.

Rathdowney had given guarantees of it was "all white money" and "no-one would lose a cent."

I did take Rathdowney's advises on face value; why wouldn't I, as he was an established practising solicitor. He assured me that he had followed up on all the legal requirements and satisfied himself that the scheme was legitimate.

There is a three-page letter written by Rathdowney to the Manager of C.K.F. Finance that succinctly states in concise detail, all what was said to me in the introduction, of the Tobjoano Scheme and how settlement was to take place, and Rathdowney's absolute guarantee of it happening. I have the letter in my possession.

On Rathdowney's advices and assurances, I deposited my funds into the Trust account of Rathdowney MacDraw: (The Trust is the Trust is the Trust). I have these receipts in my possession. Within four days I had made two deposits into Rathdowney MacDraw's Trust, totalling $100,000.000 of my money, which was my personal contribution as an investor. This supports my case that I was an independent lender.

Time after time they made what were plausible excuses for the delays, they said it's still alive and still will settle. Again the assurances are expressly stated in the letter by Rathdowney to the Manager of C.K.F. Finance.

I now have ASIC records that show Rathdowney was an Associate Director and Joana is a Director of a Holding Company of Keat-Wyatt & Associates. Keat-Wyatt & Associates were paid $112,000.00 from Rathdowney MacDraw's Trust.

After two years of excuses and no completion, I went

to the Law Society, my reason being I understood the Law Society was the Body of Authority that ruled over all solicitors and would direct Rathdowney MacDraw to account for my funds and have Rathdowney MacDraw return my personal investment held in their Trust.

The Law Society's findings were that there was insufficient evidence to support my claim. I have this ruling in my possession.

I believe through the newly established QCAT I can now as an option have the Law Society decision re-evaluated.

Not accepting the Law Society's ruling I approached the Lay Observer, who thankfully released some sketchy information regarding the Trust ledger but was obliged not to divulge the whole ledger in its entirety. I did receive very limited information that indicated the funds were transferred from the ANZ bank. I have this in my possession.

A diary note of Rathdowney's states; "I arranged the transfer of funds with Bob from the Bank."

In another letter, I challenged the Lay Observer to tell me where the funds went. With reluctance to do so, in his reply he however furnished me with how and where the funds were deposited into an individual's Bank account in Hong Kong. (This information was given to me four years after the act.) I have this in my possession.

The Lay Observer left the case open for further evidence to be presented. I have this finding of the Lay Observer in my possession.

At this time in my life I fell upon hard times and ran-out of funds to pursue the recovery of my funds fraudulently released from Rathdowney MacDraw's Trust.

I was unemployed and a breakdown of my 25-year marriage ensued.

In 1995 upon the invitation of the Lay Observer I went back to the Law Society with fresh evidence that

I was an individual investor that can be constituted by the fact that the original receipts held from Rathdowney MacDraw Trust account were un-deniably in my name.

Again, the Law Society closed ranks and my fresh submission came to no avail.

With that, and upon my strong realization of my fresh approach, being a sole investor was correct, I made a second approach to Ruck, knowing he was a solicitor of the Supreme Court and he had helped me previously in other dealings. However, at the end of the day Ruck acted contrary to my instructions and in my opinion, my solicitor, Ruck, got together with the defendant and the defendant was able to arrange with his Counsel, overnight, submissions dated the same day as the Court, and representation.

Ruck insisted on $10,000.00 being paid by me up front; two separate payments of $5000.00, only one of which I have signed an authority to release.

Ruck failed in his duty of care by working for his best interests. Examples are as follow: Extended the defendant's time to defend without my instruction.

After two years of a long-enforced waiting, causing paramount frustration on my part I began to think something was not quite right.

So, I made enquiry to the CMC about his non action.

The CMC informed that they do not investigate individuals; however, they did helpfully send me a letter with their findings that the Legal Services Commission had a case to answer regarding my complaint. (I have this in writing).

More enforced waiting after which Ruck rang me to suggest that I approach Rathdowney with an offer. My reply was NO! Rathdowney should approach me with an offer.

48 minutes later, on the same day, Rathdowney filed an application in the court to have the claim dismissed; giving me only two weeks to reply to his 63-point

Application. This was the first time in 18 years the Trust Ledger had been released by the Law Society and the first time I had the opportunity to see the Ledger.

Ruck at this point wanted <u>another</u> $5000.00 to represent me at the Hearing.

(His first action in 2 1/2 years!)

At this point I was concerned, suspicious and disillusioned about Ruck's approach thus far.

I sought by ringing the Brisbane Registry my obligation to respond to Rathdowney's Application.

I was advised of my course of action to make my response by affidavit, and to turn up on the day for the Hearing set down to be in Chambers. (As per the Court File, that which I have in my possession).

Knowing I could not raise ANOTHER $5000.00 and armed with the information from the Registry I emailed Ruck on the 18 of May 2009; and my instructions to him were, "NO INTERM ACTIONS, or APPLICATIONS ARE REQUIRED. (I have this email in my possession)

I believe the extra $5000.00 was a strategy to rule me out.

Ruck for the rest of the week bomb-barded me with demands for THAT extra $5000.00. He went to such lengths to send someone to my postal address and pinned a note to the door demanding I phone Ruck. This note I have in my possession.

I, believing the Court closed at 4.30 each day and therefore there was no further business for that day, I emailed Ruck again believing the Court File that was posted, would stand, and the Hearing would be held in Chambers as listed. I have that document in my possession and stamped by the Court.

From this point on I avoided all communication because I knew I had to face the chamber hearing the next day, feeling un-bolstered and unsupported by my solicitor, I knew I had no other choice but to represent myself as it was set-down for a Hearing by affidavit and not a trial.

After shutting down communication, Ruck, unusually enough sent an email to me with submissions I believe were inadmissible. Too late! (I have these in my possession). Further documents were sent by him on the Monday after Court.

I arrived at the Courts on the Friday, May 2009, and checked the notice board to find the Chamber Hearing had been moved to an open Court. I went to the Court early and the Court Clerk commented that there was a solicitor going to hook up with the Court at 10 am.

To my utter surprise it was Ruck that had rung the Court to organise the hook-up by telephone with the Court.

It was Ruck, himself, ringing from up North, after having been instructed not to interfere with the process.

He opened, whilst not on record, he called the judge by Christian name. Over the loud speakers I heard Ruck tell the Court he was here "to remind the Court that the submissions that I, (he, Ruck) had emailed Mr Jan Ernest Gainsworthy(me) were not admissible as evidence." (I have in my possession the Court Transcripts.)

Informed by Registry that it was to be by affidavit in Chambers I was taken aback by the presence of Rathdowney, who was to represent himself at the Hearing, had with him, a barrister, C. Douglas SC, and another solicitor, P. Black, as his legal support.

I believe Ruck phoned Rathdowney after I had notified Ruck that I would be representing myself, the night BEFORE the Court. How else would Rathdowney know to engage a barrister and have submissions to present, when it was on the Court File that it was a Hearing to be held in Chambers by affidavit?

Rathdowney's barrister submitted a wad of paperwork that was dated the same day as the Court, clearly to me now that they were made up, after 4:30 pm the night before, or, on the morning of the Court. (I have this in my possession).

After this point it took the Judge six days in all to bring down her Order. I have this in my possession.

Two hours later she amended the Order due to what was described as a spelling mistake. Still, the error persists in the order. (Mistake: Third spelt as second)

To add insult to injury and after the event, Ruck sent to me a Statement of Claim with DRAFT written on it, for the sum of $2000.00.

I have copies in my possession.

Subsequent attempts for justice by me have been thwarted. I have these in my possession.

If you feel you are unable to help me, could you please refer me to someone you feel may be able to help me.

Yours sincerely

Jan Ernest Gainsworthy

Upon reflection, the above letters written in July 2011 show the pent-up emotion and frustration I was suffering at the time. Parts now seem to me to be incoherent and irrational, with ramblings of poor English. I was indignant at being ignored and very, very angry that the authorities had wiped the floor with me. They were not willing to lift a finger to arrive at the truth.

I could not conceive of the denial and lies that befell me, directed from those in the ivory towers, the anointed ones with the power to act. Although a 20 per cent response is good by advertising standards, they all had the same two underlying issues to throw back on me.

First were the inhibitive upfront costs—the money. To have the slightest chance of success, a suit would cost thousands in legal representation fees, with no guarantees. By making any legal action cost-prohibitive to clients, lawyers and barristers selectively excuse themselves from being involved in cases with little return.

It's a cop-out for true justice. A facade that sees many innocent people suffer injustices because of the legal fraternity's cost-prohibitive tactics.

The second evasive action is to take what money you have, string you out, and come back to get more money to take you to the next step.

An outcome is always around the corner but just out of reach. The carrot and donkey principle.

The illusion is created to make you think they are doing everything to arrive at a just outcome. It is nothing more than smoke and mirrors. After all, the likely outcome is a well-guarded secret from the clients yet known by both parties' solicitors and barristers from the outset.

To appeal a decision is in the same vein. The outcome has been determined. That's my personal experience of the Queensland legal system.

I found it to be iniquitous, far from the halls of a transparent justice system.

Second was their observation that "Jan, you have had your day in court, and an order has been handed down."

That is the system's take on the contrived outcome. The order in my case was a travesty of transparent justice. To hide the corrupt proceedings, my case will be buried in the state archives, preserved forever as just one of many that has been dealt with by authorities with the inscription of "We're not going there."

Another brick in the wall, cemented by injustice.

So be it! However, faith is the substance of things not yet seen.

Never, ever give up on your dreams. Nobody is allowed to know what is around the corner because that would undo trust in the one authority on earth and undermine faith itself.

"Don't ever give up" is the edict!

CHAPTER 4

Stonewalled

For nine months I had put all my faith in a positive outcome of the appeal to the federal executive council in the Australian Parliament; hopeful that after this appeal had been tabled by my local federal member, Vladimir Rossi, and supported by the gun barrister on his team, Senator Bill Gillard, the ordeal would be terminated.

I believed that cracks were beginning to appear in the stonewall of the Queensland legal system—the wall protecting those anointed ones, now cowled down, cloistered, and having closed ranks on the inside. All were hoping that just maybe, Jan Ernest Gainsworthy would go away, and they would not have to suffer the humiliation of having light shed on their involvement, which would soil their reputations.

Ignited by my legal challenge to have the solicitor account for invested trust funds, the authorities had blotted their copybooks. What was to ensue was a dodgy, contrived legal outcome that no one in the legal system can endorse. The court order cannot be validated by the rule of law; to save face, the fraternity has denied and now must discard the evidence by burying it in the archives, forever.

Nine months later came the renderers, the Wit brothers, to patch the cracks. They were Dim Wit and Half Wit respectively: the federal MP Vladimir Rossi and Senator Gillard. With sleight of hand and a one-page letter from Gillard to Rossi, Gillard used Rossi as a human shield from my wrath. The senator, devoid of duty of care, wriggled out of what I believed to be his non-delegable duty to act on a crime put before him. I was aghast at the insipid and mediocre response. Its intention was to plaster over the cracks and make things look new, justifying the Queensland legal system's trumped-up, seamless stance.

The senator, the shadow attorney general, being an anointed one of the Queensland legal system, plugged up the gaping holes of the Queensland legal system with a whopper by saying that "Mr Gainsworthy understands that the principal of the independency of the courts prevent me, as Shadow Attorney-General, from commenting upon decisions handed down by the Brisbane District Court or the Court of Appeal."

The response was yet another political whitewash. A very shallow response indeed, which excused Bill Gillard from state jurisdiction. The senator avoided, at all cost, any federal duty of care implied as the incumbent of his office. The senator mentioned nothing of the High Court, nothing of the federal executive to which the appeal was directed. Senator Gillard would be alive to the avenue available and the procedural correctness of how to assist with my application.

I, Jan Gainsworthy, being beleaguered and not accepting for one minute the argument that the senator, a gun barrister, was not in the position to assist, made further application to the Australian Federal Police with the hope that they may well look into Rathdowney's shady past.

I sent a covering letter and the whole file to the Australian Federal Police in Canberra, believing there were associated crimes by Joana and Rathdowney against the Commonwealth which fell into the jurisdiction of the AFP.

The covering letter is posted below.

Jan Ernest Gainsworthy

5th June 2012

Australia Federal Police
AOCC Client Liaison Team
Canberra   ACT 2601

Dear Sirs

I make this official submission of crimes, to the Australian Federal Police as I believe it falls under the AFP jurisdiction of Commonwealth fraud, in the areas of money laundering and organised crime.

I allege, without prejudice, that individuals of the Queensland legal system and State Government have closed ranks to deny me justice by covering up the criminal acts of a practicing solicitor, Joe Noel Rathdowney and his partner Kevin Joana, (Clive Kerry Fletcher).

The secrecy and cover-up by the Queensland legal system is akin to organised crime. My conspiracy theory conjured them having banded together to conceal the truth.

Neither one authority, nor individual has acted in accordance of the laws and their jurisdiction. Instead they have flagrantly ignored the facts of a crime that each has had put before them.

In my expose' detailing Rathdowney's trail of deceit, (pages, 118 & 119 of my indexed paginated bundle), I have illustrated beyond any reasonable doubt, that Mr Rathdowney has had the protection of individuals of the Queensland legal system which has allowed this trail of deceit to go untethered for more than twenty years.

As early as 2005, I approached the Queensland Law Society and admonished that Rathdowney was involved in laundering money overseas. My embezzled funds from the trust account of Rathdowney MacDraw were deposited into an individual's Hong Kong bank account. Details are contained in my letter dated, 27th January 2009, to my then solicitor Sean Ruck. (Attached.)

Yet the QLS have on record, the money distribution, as far back as 1993.

I believe the Queensland Law Society had a non-delegable duty to notify the Australian Federal Police of the situation, when it was known to them in 1993. Mr Rathdowney has never accounted for these funds released without authority from his law firm's trust account, a blatant breach of the trust rules.

The moneys released from the trust of Rathdowney MacDraw without authorities and specifics, are contrary to the Trust Account Act. I contend that the QLS would have been in the position to know of Mr Rathdowney's priors.

Mr Rathdowney conjoined by company directorship, with his business partner Kevin Joana (Clive Francis Fletcher) in 2009, sent off-shore moneys to Europe, the embezzled funds of Dundas ($2.4 million), a retired farmer, that had trusted Joana's word, "that he (KJ) would get him (Dundas) good interest ". A scam, similar to what the pair did in 1990 to me and others.

I have approached the Crime and Misconduct Commission, another Queensland overseeing body that has seemingly sat on their hands and not brought the Commissioner of the Queensland Legal Services Commission, Bob Jenkins to account for their non-specific performance.

I have uncovered the fact that Frank Davidson of the Queensland Law Society Inc., withheld crucial evidence of Rathdowney MacDraw's trust ledger that substantiates Rathdowney had an invested interest as Associate director to Kevin Joana, his partner, not his client.

The Company, Keat-Wyatt & Associates was the 'advisory' arm, of C. K. F.Finance Co and Kevin Joana was the Managing director. (Clive Kerry Fletcher).

Keat-Wyatt & Associates were paid from Rathdowney MacDraw's trust account over a period, $112, 000.00. (Evidenced on the trust ledger)

These facts were not brought to light until Frank Davidson released the documents held by the QLS to Rathdowney for him (JNR) to make application to strike out our claim in 2009.

The Queensland Legal Services Commission too, are covering up a fraud, and have allowed Rathdowney, having two indictments, to continue practising law, at will, within the community and to operate "offshore investments," in partnership with Joana & Ors, to defraud the Commonwealth of taxable income, for their own gain and enrichment.

The Commissioner Jenkins has covered-up the fact that Frank Davidson withheld the Trust Ledger and other vital information such as Rathdowney's diary note (17/07/1990) on how the trust funds were released without written authority from the beneficiaries.

Another "Bob" from the ANZ bank released the trust funds without having written authority from the beneficiaries of the trust. It was merely released on Rathdowney's say so.

Accordingly, the ANZ bank is responsible, and should show cause, why the funds were released without authorities.

Who has the authority and power to bury two indictments in the Queensland State Archives for sixty-five years? And then go on to practice law.

The State of Queensland is culpable of covering up a crime and prescribing and precluding me from justice. It is the most basic tenant of Government; to protect individuals within society from injustice.

This is another reason I see the Australian Federal Police are the authority to pull up a rogue Queensland State and oversee justice according to the Commonwealth and Australia Constitution. In no other State or Territory would I have been so severely prejudiced by a legal system that has flouted the written law and denied me natural justice.

In my research, I found that the whole file in the Court records of the case;

Devine –V- Rathdowney & Anor File No. PLT1315/93 had been destroyed, yet, not been archived.

Rathdowney was the defendant in a claim for damages, about the time he was indicted.

Who has the authority to destroy public Court records without being recorded in the archives?

I believe there are traces of insider interference, within the Courts, contrary to the rules. Fraud.

The general public have been exposed to criminals without warning from the authorities that have the responsibility to protect them.

Ruck, a Supreme Court solicitor, manipulated the Courts and changed a scheduled Chamber hearing into an open Court, thus changing the Chair and allowing him to appear by telephone to pervert the course of justice. So too did Cameron Douglas SC, appear on that day as the defendant's counsel and Douglas SC tabled a wad of documents dated the same day as the Court, which is not allowed by the rules. By his criminal action, and defending a felon, Cameron Douglas SC further perverted the course of natural justice.

Also, I made official complaint against Rathdowney to my local CIB.

Upon the CMC's investigation, they found no trace of this whole file either.

It simply vanished with no record. It could be that one of Rathdowney's indictments was from my official complaint. I am unable to establish that fact because of the sixty-five year caveat placed on the file held by the Queensland Archives.

Item Nos. are listed on page 119 of my indexed paginated bundle.

I approached the recently formed Queensland Public Interest Clearing House but they have stone walled me like every other Queensland Government Department.

My recent approach on advices from the Queen's senior correspondent was to contact my local Federal MP, Vladimir Rossi, son of Virgil Rossi, the only judge to be sacked by the Queensland Parliament, after the Fritzer Inquiry.

I had asked Vladimir Rossi MP to table my submission and affidavit in the Australian Parliament and have it reviewed by The Federal Executive Council. Definitively, Rossi was my voice in the Australian Parliament. However, MP Rossi did not table my submission but passed it on to Sen. Bill Gillard, Shadow Attorney General.

After seven months, suspended in time, I then approached my neighbouring MP R. Krammer to table my submission in the Australian Parliament. I have received nothing from Katter's office. He too is a Queenslander.

Nine months later Senator Gillard responded with a negative; he could not assist, saying it was not within his jurisdiction.

This to the writer was a fabricated excuse, a little white lie that senator Gillard had not the position to act and act appropriately. If that were to be true; then why string the writer out for *nine* months?

The responses of Rossi and Gillard are also attached.

I contend that both are Queenslanders protecting their power and covering for the individuals of the Queensland legal system, which by way of misfeasance have obstructed and perverted the course of natural justice and covered up a crime relating to the Commonwealth.

By Rossi's and Gillard' responses they have gagged me and denied me the right of freedom of speech, subsequently allowing a known felon (Rathdowney) to go free and practise law at will, leaving the Public uninformed and vulnerable to his and Joana's Bottom of the Harbour' schemes.

It is illegitimate, for a decision maker to be biased and to withhold public information.

I believe, Senator Gillard, on receiving my submission, should have contacted the Australian

Federal Police, and alerted the AFP to the unchecked corruption.

I find Senator Gillard's inaction, derelict of his duty of Office and responsibilities.

This is yet, another cover-up of the crimes put before the two men, Rossi and Gillard.

I can only surmise that Senator Gillard did not act appropriately because he is a barrister, one of the Queensland legal system's 'brothers in arms'.

Senator Gillard too, should have tabled my submission in the Senate for the Federal Executive and not made personal judgement of my case. As an individual he had neither the power nor the authority to be judge and jury over my claim and seal my fate; ignoring my direction to put it before the Federal Executive. It was not to be a one-man call.

I had also written to the then Attorney General of Queensland, Patrick Luckless who also refused to act on my pleadings.

The Governor General, (a Queenslander with a law background) has refused to act on a directive of the Queen to look into my plea for clemency.

I contend that if the Queensland authorities had acted appropriately in 1993, then Dundas, the retired farmer, would have not been victim to the exploitation of Joana and Rathdowney, who scammed $2.4 M from Dundas. Kevin Joana moved the money off-shore, this time to Europe.

Again, the purpose of shifting funds off-shore was to conceal the money trail by nominating bogus investor banks and a contrived broker, Mr Dick.

The embezzled funds sent off-shore defrauded the Commonwealth with the intention for Joana and Rathdowney to make personal gain and enrichment.

I have written and published a book, *Without Prejudice*.

Included is a copy for the AFP file.

I believe the Queensland legal system will try to

block the truth that is contained in my book that was published in the USA.

I am grateful for your audience. My expressed wish is that the Australian Federal Police examine these Commonwealth crimes contained in my submission and force the Queensland legal authorities to be accountable for my long and enforced waiting for justice.

I thank you for your fullest considerations.

Yours faithfully

Jan Ernest Gainsworthy

The whole file and my book were returned within a month with an accompanying letter. In a nutshell, the Australian Federal Police said,

"Therefore, the AFP is not the correct agency for your complaint submission." They suggested alternative means, but I had been on that wheel. It was a door and chapter closed. So be it. I had been stonewalled.

CHAPTER 5

From a Death, New Beginnings

With my shift of consciousness brought about by the recent sudden passing of Steven R., I felt somehow relieved that the Australian Federal Police and the Crime and Misconduct Commission had closed my case.

Their responses were to me a load off. Instantly, my high levels of anxiety dropped significantly. I was no longer focused on an expected outcome. There was now no second-guessing, no what ifs. For the first time in years, I stopped thinking of what my next step might be. I stopped going to bed worrying how to end the nightmare.

It was my answered prayer. Tobjoano, the loan's swindle, which had been the bane of my life for two decades, was over; just let it go. The only one holding on to any part of this saga was me. However, I have no regrets in pursuing what I believed to be my truth. Hopefully, lesson learned. A new beginning was an opportunity to change my focus and live the rest of my life without being embroiled in legal argument, having no professional support.

To everybody and agency, they saw my argument as crying over spilt milk. I simply couldn't grasp their shallow findings. I was arguing on the grounds of principle: "A trust is a trust is a trust! And it was my bloody milk!"

Again, I was to invoke the Serenity Prayer. The situation after twenty-two years was one I could not change. I had, as an individual, to the best of my ability, pursued the resolution to this saga by the letter of the law. I had not made threats nor acted in any manner that could be construed as inappropriate. Yet I found myself isolated from the general populace.

My plight was akin to trying to sue city hall. "Good luck with justice, Jan!" was the cry from the masses.

I will never agree with the court's decisions, never! Nor will I agree with the findings of the authorities. But I now accept, wholly, that the saga is over. Tobjoano is finished.

I shall on the completion of this book, *Those in Ivory Towers*, dust myself off and seek a brighter future. This will be my final book, closure on what was a horror patch of my life. It is a pyrrhic victory, something that now makes me smile. Remember, laughter is the best medicine. I look back at the overwhelming struggle for what I thought was my justice and ask myself, "What was I thinking?"

Somehow, though, I still believe it was part of my fate and destiny, my karma, my task to do and lesson to learn in this lifetime. Then I say to myself, "Chores are done; all is well, Jan."

Philosophically, I understand that the anointed ones too have had a pyrrhic victory. The authorities may well have covered for Rathdowney, yet at what price? Their deeds have been exposed and written onto the pages of my books. These deeds cannot be undone by simple denial. These deeds are what determine the outcomes of the wheel of fortune, karma. How can conscience argue right when one has sold out on integrity? Who among the anointed ones can ever draw legal argument and say, "Jan Ernest Gainsworthy was treated fairly as to his birthright and the Australia Constitution"? And too, how can the learned ladies and gentlemen called to the bar dispute my contention that being ordered to pay court costs to the felon, Joe Noel Rathdowney, the solicitor who defrauded me, was not malice? I rest my case, Your Honours. Cynically, I goad the judges and justices by directly avowing, "You, Your Honours, be the judges on my verdicts and disputation."

One of my greatest lessons learned was to recognize that any success gained is, from the outset, a risk: there is no such thing as a sure thing. There are few absolutes in our universe, such as the speed of light. No one knows what tomorrow may bring. Uncertainty abounds; stresses and worry make for a hard pillow. But I have found in all my adversity that having faith the size of a mustard seed will get you through. Faith is the hope of all things not yet seen. Never say never, and never, ever give up.

Despite all the negative findings and the ghastly outcome, I know there is only one authority on earth. I have it on good authority that justice is served as God ordains. To overcome adversity is not for the faint-hearted. Everybody has a set of rules to live by, and everybody is accountable for the choices they make. As I said in chapter 2, "No one escapes the wheel of fortune; no one gets out of this life alive."

Time and words are similar in that neither can be retrieved. There is no going back to the good old days. The only thing you get to keep in this world are your words, and the only thing you may take is a photograph.

CHAPTER 6

Unicameralism

While accepting that the long, drawn-out saga was over, and the track had turned out to be a dead end, I still had unsettling thoughts of how it all came about. How was it that no one would stand up for what I believed to be a simple civil claim of money owing from a law firm's trust?

By the rules, it was for the authorities to have my invested funds accounted for, legally. Then, by court order, the investment funds would be returned to me in full. If there was non-compliance by the trustee, then the trustee would be held accountable. The trustee would be struck off and the beneficiary's funds covered by the Solicitor's Indemnity Fund.

I wondered what drove the establishment into denial, and how individuals had the power to dismiss a legitimate case. How could the Queensland legal system refute my pleadings and not act in accordance with their written laws?

"Unfortunately," the reply I had received on a few occasions, was not a legal determination, nor a concise order of a legal proceeding. "Unfortunately," used in their context to me, was a cop-out, a term to excuse individuals of their responsibility.

Still, the nagging question: How did the authorities get away with such a contemptuous whitewash?

I now believe the answer lies within the structure of *unicameralism*—a term that is relatively new to me, a word that means "with one legislative chamber."

I have previously made comment that I believe Queensland to be a rogue state, having selective allegiance to the Australia Constitution. Unicameralism was the reason for the Queensland State's lack of adherence to the constitution.

Queensland is the only state that does not have an upper house of parliament. That allows the state's premier to censure the whole of the Queensland Parliament. It provides an unruly avenue for one individual to push bills through the parliament with little or no debate, annihilating opposition undemocratically.

Unicameralism at its inception had that intention. The then-Labor premier, Edward Granville Theodore, nicknamed "Red Ted," in 1920 had yet another rejection by the legislative council of a bill to increase pastoral rent, which triggered his push to have the upper house abolished in 1921. It's incredible that one man could stack the numbers of the House, which had been duly elected, and then have the members vote themselves out. Thereafter, Queensland was robbed of true democracy. The Labor party in 1934, further cemented unicameralism, by making an amendment to the bill, such that the only way the upper house could be restored was by way of a peoples' referendum. Knowing the "Queenslanders" mindset, that will never happen! It follows, democratic opposition was annihilated from 1921, and the fair process of the checks and balances of an upper house removed, intentionally forever.

Having only one chamber robs the Queensland people of checks and balances, provided by an upper chamber, which by constitution allows for freedom of speech and democratic convention to govern "fairly" for its constituents. Even the village idiot is to have a say and be treated fairly in a true democracy, but this is unattainable in Queensland because of autonomous rule.

I realised too that this was how Joh Bjelke Petersen was able to wield his personal power and create what I call a 'police state'.

I am situated five kilometres from the Queensland/New South Wales border, and I head north to travel to work in the sunshine state. Crossing from New South Wales to Queensland, there exists a sign saying, "Welcome to Queensland."

Often, only one kilometre inside the sunshine state, there is a speed camera or a policeman in a highway pursuit car, stopped in the centre island of the carriageway, pointing a speed gun at motorists heading north. That's the welcome!

Years ago, when I was driving my Ford Laser to work, I was for some unremembered reason belting down in the outside lane, perhaps a little over the speed limit (in a 100 kilometre per hour zone). I looked up and spotted the policeman with a speed gun pointed at my vehicle. I jabbed the brakes three or four times to decelerate quickly. By the time I passed the police officer with the speed gun, my estimated travelling speed was no more than ninety-five kilometres per hour. I indicated and moved over to the left-hand lane of the dual carriageway.

I thought, *Phew! That was close,* and merrily went on my way. Leaving the motorway, I took exit 87, nine kilometres from where the officer was checking speeds.

I had just left the motorway at exit 87 when, in my rear-view mirror, I spotted the highway pursuit car barrelling over the crest. *Shit!* I thought, *he's coming down the off-ramp, after me.* In an instant he was on my rear.

The policeman followed me for a couple of kilometres, now in a built-up area and a speed limit of sixty-kilometres per hour. I kept the little blue Laser in third gear and drove most sedately. I indicated to turn left at the T-intersection at Scottsdale Drive. The police pursuit vehicle turned right. As I glanced over, the policeman gave me the "royal salute." Some call it the Hawaiian wave, others the finger or the bird. I thought, *Go and catch a real crook like Rathdowney, Ruck, or C. Douglas, you clown.*

Queensland has always been a police state to me, and events in history illustrate it.

In no other state or territory of the Commonwealth of Australia can the premier, as an individual, have so much muscle without checks and balances.

It is ludicrous! Far from the halls of good governance for the people who voted the party in. It is simply a blight on democracy that amounts to cronyism. Present day, we see our new premier wielding the axe on government departments, changing legislation overnight, without consultation, to rob workers of their entitlements. It is outrageous to me that one person can be given so much power and effectively have free rein over the lives of all constituents.

Queensland, since the founding of the federation and prior too, has been the defiant state. Only when Queensland knew the other states were unanimously agreed upon forming a federation did Queensland agree to be part.

As far back as 1834, before federation, Queensland failed to comply with the British Empire's official act in relation to the abolition of slavery.

The Abolition of Slavery Act was passed in 1833.

From the 1860s, Queensland, as a free-governing British colony, attached by great distance, had a demand for labourers to work the sugar cane farms. Circumventing the Abolition of Slavery Act, Queensland adopted the practice of what became to be known as *blackbirding*. Blackbirding was recruitment of non-European labourers from the islands to the north of Australia, such as the Solomon's and Vanuatu. As slavery was illegal, the recruited labourers were officially labelled "indentured." It was a Queensland authoritarian sleight of hand.

While some labourers were willing to be blackbirded, there were many others who were tricked or forced against their will onto the blackbirding ships, which then set sail for the cane fields of Queensland. This practice of blackbirding continued in Queensland for a period of forty years, even after President Lincoln had called for the abolition of slavery in the United States in the mid-1860s, and in the knowledge that there was an official British act outlawing slavery.

Aboriginals were also indentured in this period from Cape York, to be put to work on the southern cane farms.

The brief history of blackbirding above is to illustrate the sheer lack of moral integrity that was ingrained in the administration of the Queensland colony over a century and a half ago.

More recently, in 1934, the first batch of 101 cane toads arrived at the breeding station near Gordonvale, Queensland. The toads were caught in Hawaii by Benjamin Montrose of the Bureau of Sugar Research. Everyone is aware of the environmental devastation these toads have caused since. Queensland has not been held accountable for the environmental vandalism affecting our native species; this spill of cane toads is as severe as an oil slick, spreading Australia-wide, killing native fauna and pets. I contend the Queensland government should be indicted for creating such an environmental disaster. Again, silence has combined with no action, nor any responsibility taken by the Queensland government for introducing such a destructive pest.

The spill of these toads is as great a disaster as the Exxon Valdez oil spill, after the oil tanker hit a reef in the remote Prince William Sound in 1989.

These toads are still oozing from the state of Queensland and have found their way to Darwin, Kakadu, and as far west as Kununurra.

I contend too that very little has changed. There is an underlying, ongoing pattern of silence, with no action or responsibility taken by the Queensland government. Still, to this day it acts as a free colony, ignoring the monarch's decrees and undermining our forefathers' precious constitution.

I am alarmed by the lack of integrity that persists within the governing bodies of Queensland and that has been allowed to snowball, unchecked, for decades. I maintain that in no other Commonwealth state or territory of Australia would I, as a constituent, have been treated so unfairly. Nevertheless, I have resolved to drop my case, having the understanding that there have been far greater injustices dealt by the Queensland state than the one I have had to endure.

One does not have to dig deeply; just scratch the surface and there can be found atrocities that far outweigh my experience of injustice. Those injustices handed out by the powers that be, the anointed ones, have been covering up wrongful actions for centuries. It happens, I postulate, because they think they can, and because the anointed ones mistakenly think they are above the law.

Meanwhile, the instigators and manipulators of unicameralism stay silent. They are the lawmakers, together with the lawbreakers, and the madness of inequality and injustice is perpetuated.

Let us go back. First, there were the Kanakas, some of whom were kidnapped against their will. It was the Australia Federal Parliament (not Queensland), after federation, that put in place the Pacific Island Labours Act of 1902 and repatriated the islanders.

Queensland had to follow suit because they were now in the federation. It was not their call. Queensland was obliged to adopt the rules of the Commonwealth, and most likely the Commonwealth bailed them out financially.

An atrocity that the Queensland government buried, "a story that should be told again and again," according to Professor Rob Britzer's feature article in the *Weekend Australia* newspaper, March 19–20 2011, is that of an MP. The article was titled "The St Patrick's Day bashing of people's champion: An extremely serious assault on a dissident MP was greeted with official silence."

I concur with Britzer's admonishment that the story needs to be told again and again, so I have transcribed excerpts of the article to paint the picture of unruly government:

> SAINT Patrick's Day 1949, marks one of the most infamous incidents in Australia political history.
>
> On that day, Australia's first and only Communist Party MP, Joel Wendell Peterson, was savagely bashed by a plainclothes policeman – almost certainly on the direct orders of authoritarian ALP state premier E.M. (Noel) Hanson.
>
> Yet, in the ALP-controlled Queensland of the late 40s, an extremely serious assault upon a dissident member of parliament was greeted with an extraordinary official silence.
>
> To add insult to injury, in 1950 – at the behest of Hanson and the Queensland ALP – Peterson's seat of Howden was deliberately redistributed out of existence.
>
> "The story of this action, and the bashing of other people on this day, is one that should be told again and again, to expose the corruption of some members of the police force and the corruption of some government administrators."
>
> Vale Joel Peterson. Lest we forget.

Professor Rob Britzer is author of thirty-seven books, and I found his account of the "bashing of the people's champion" chilling. It pales my story into insignificance.

It is a documented, true account of how Queensland, in particular, has been the rogue state of the federation, and illustrates abuse of power due to unicameralism. Further too, a recent newspaper article elucidated the ongoing cover-up of the Queensland government and official silence in relation to the pack rape of fourteen-year-old (at the time) Anita Murray, twenty-two years ago.

Upon reading the feature article in the *Weekend Australia* newspaper, 21–22 August 2011, by Shane Smith, and upon the recent passing of Stephen R., I, Jan Ernest Gainsworthy, now capitulate.

Smith's article illustrates further the contempt and cronyism of Queensland authorities and their unruly arrogance in regard to justice.

Again, I invite, "You to be the judge."

The article was headed "Two decades on and a search for justice in the Hinze Affair continues." I have extracted excerpts and included them in the body of this work to compare and contrast the players' modus operandi in both games.

> AN extraordinary document has been lodged with Queensland's Child Protection Commission of inquiry and released to the public. In support of an application for the Commissioner to recuse himself, it includes unsubstantiated claims that there may be sufficient cause for the Governor General Britany Kwong and six serving Queensland judicial officers to be investigated for possible breaches of Section 87 of the Queensland Criminal Code, relating to official corruption.
>
> The report also makes similar claims against Commissioner Tom McCardle SC, a former Commissioner of the Queensland Crime Commission and many other senior figures in the Queensland legal and public service establishment.
>
> At its initial hearing on July 17, (2012) Commissioner McCardle was asked to recuse himself by Lindsborg's lawyer, Mitchel Bosch, and former journalist Brice Gandy on the grounds he had failed to act after extensive coverage in The Curious Mail of the abuse, and an official complaint lodged with the QCC when he was commissioner in 2001.
>
> Commissioner McCardle decided not to step aside, ruling that the QCC was not a part of the Queensland government, which he interpreted as "the political executive; that is the Premier and Cabinet."
>
> Hinze is about an injustice, compounded by a cover-up which remains unexplored.

Those submissions are now publicly held and appear to show that all members of the Boss cabinet on March 5, 1990, and certain public officials knew that the "public records" were required as evidence when they ordered and carried out their secret shedding on March 23, 1990.

The QCMC dismissed the request citing, inter alia, "staleness" and saying it was not in the "public interest."

The writer has over the years been staved off by the authorities using the same stale arguments as "staleness" and "not in the public interest." And the writer agrees also with, Tibb's view and addressing the "staleness" point, said: "Under the circumstances, we suggest any claim of 'staleness' or 'lack of public interest' which may be mounted now by Queensland authorities not to revisit this matter ought fail.

Anita Murray, the young rape victim at the sad heart of this matter, still wants justice.

The Hinze Affair is now content studied internationally by students undertaking courses in government accountability.

For Murray, a 14 year old at the time of the attack, the cover-up and the injustice has continued long enough.

Smith's feature article is an extraordinary account which highlights anomalies of the legal system and the politicians' sleight of hand to avoid being responsible for the choices they make behind closed doors in their ivory towers.

Many points Smith makes are a living reality to me. I am still gobsmacked that not even the findings of the High Court Chief Justice, Gary Tibbs, and Ors can motivate the Queensland authorities to come clean and act according to the laws of this nation. If one joins the dots Smith points to, then it can be clearly seen that all is not squeaky clean in the halls of the Queensland Parliament, nor in the courts of this unicameral state.

Truly, I would not have gone to such lengths in pursuit of justice if I had known the extent of corruption in the ivory towers, crawling with "grinning rats with a gold tooth." From the outset my pursuit of justice was all but false hope. It's time to laugh at this crazy situation. Who would have thought it would take twenty-two years for the muddy water to clear? But given time, the muddiest of waters does become clear.

This final outcome was indeed not how I had imagined nor wished. Although I will never back down from my claim, it is obvious that there is nowhere this can go.

My books are a cathartic expression of the experience. The intention behind publishing my story is to at least have a say and detach from the emotional frustration; to walk away, knowing all that could be done, as an individual, was done.

Bill Gates listed eleven rules to living in this world, none of which I totally agree with, but again, I have capitulated and bow momentarily to the worldly nonsense.

Gates' number one rule is "Life isn't fair. Get used to it!"

I am guessing Gates made that rule up to justify having attained an unimaginable and inordinate amount of individual wealth. And it is conceivable truth, compelling coming from Bill Gates. But to me, Gates's rule is far short of what life is.

Mostly, people don't challenge Gates's first rule; they merely nod their heads and say, "Yes, that's how it is for me."

After my drubbing by the courts, it would be easy to side with Gates's view.

However, more than ever, I am convinced that we get everything in life we ask for: karma. Life is fair. Life, too, is precious. I suggest you care. I suggest you take an interest in local community and government, because it is the power belonging to the peoples of the world that brings about change.

"Life was not meant to be easy but can be delightful" (W.C. Fields).

I would add, "Life was meant to be fair and joyful. Stick with the programme!"

Never give up! No one knows what's around the corner.

CHAPTER 7

The Now and Where To?

After yielding to the stonewalled responses—despondent, but now willing to start again by leaving that entire wake of Tobjoano in the past—I thought, *What's next?*

I immediately reflected on the therapeutic benefits of my trip to the far north of Australia.

I remembered the freedom of not being tethered to the daily grind of nine-to-five and having no compliance to the banks. I set off in the second week of February 2011. I was off on my adventure, 2011 being my planned gap year. I travelled 40,000 kilometres over a period of seven months. February was far too early to travel to the centre, so my first stop was in the foothills of the Victorian snow country, a couple of hours from Melbourne, to see an old work buddy from the Gold Coast.

Then it was on to the Blue Mountains, New South Wales, to catch up with my cousin, whom I had not seen for thirty-five years. After a time, there in low-lying cloud and drizzle, I traversed the New South Wales border to the rain-drenched Riverina, across the sodden Mallee country to Renmark, South Australia. I stayed with another dear friend in Adelaide for a couple of weeks, with the weather being picture-perfect. I left the fine weather behind, along with the city and its entire people, heading in northerly direction from Adelaide.

The sunny pleasant weather was not to return until seven or eight weeks later. I had planned to take more time tracking across the Flinders Rangers, but because of the gloomy weather forecasts, I pushed through to Tenant Creek. The desert was green; Lake Ore was 80 per cent full, from unprecedented rains for the second year in a row. I drove the treacherous Oodnadatta Track. I stood on the southern edge of Lake Ore, gazing at the vastness, thinking the only way to comprehend this inland lake, metres below sea level, was to fly over it. Perhaps I could have avoided the discomfort of a wet Oodnadatta Track.

Committed though, I met the bitumen again at Martha, then on to Tennent Creek. The weather had turned sour. It was now pouring with rain, so much so that I considered it too wet to set up camp. I took a motel room for the night.

Next day was on to Alice Springs, where I pitched the tent for a longer stay.

My goal was to travel to Arnhem Land in the Northern Territory at the end of the wet season. Yet, I had not allowed for the extension to the duration of the normal wet season and could not conceive of the volume of tropical rain.

The weather was patchy for the Alice, still raining every other day, so I thought to fill in some time. I would revisit Katherine and Darwin, with the expectation to head to Arnhem Land at the end of May or start of June.

I had not been to Darwin since the June after Cyclone Tracey, 1975.

The city had been rebuilt. I found very little change apart from the spreading housing estates. The Darwinians' focus was still on the Japanese air raids, Cyclone Tracey, and crocodiles.

My stay was brief before then driving south to Katherine Gorge. I had not been in this part of the world either for thirty-five years.

Katherine Gorge National Park, where I camped, had been given back to the native Aboriginals, the traditional land owners, and it now had taken on their original name Nitmiluk. Nitmiluk George is just a splendid part of the world, and I was happy to bushwalk and get back to nature.

The campground at Nitmiluk was soggy from the persistent, unprecedented wet season. A national park ranger told me they had had a prolonged wet season, dumping three and a half metres of rain. Obviously, the reason I could not get access to Arnhem Land; roads were cut and under metres of water.

To kill time, I pointed the van north-west to Kununurra, then to Derby. I then went further west to Port Headland, where the temperature dropped to seventeen-degrees Celsius; I decided not to venture any further south. Also, I made the decision I could not live in the harsh mining environment of Port Headland. It was male dominated, with coal road-trains passing through the centre of town. I took another slant on the interpretation of FIFO: fight your way in and fight your way out.

Within three days, I turned the van around and headed back toward Broome.

I propped and set up camp at Eighty Mile Beach on the Indian Ocean, 280 kilometres south-west of Broome. The same day, Mick from Melbourne pulled in to the caravan/camp park, and he did likewise: setting up his campsite one hundred metres away.

Mick had left Melbourne, giving a day's notice to family and friends that he was off, travelling to the far north Australian. Mick had purchased a second-hand Jeep and was towing a five-by-three trailer that he had modified by mounting a pop-up tent on it. I was envious because it would take him only fifteen minutes to set up or pack up, whereas I took an hour loading or unloading the van to pitch the tent.

Mick had quite a presence: a rough, hillbilly appearance, long beard, and earrings. In fact, Mick later divulged he was a member of a notorious bikie group.

Mick's mates thought he was a little effeminate, having stepped off his Harley Davidson motorbike to drive a Jeep Cherokee. Effeminate, Mick was not. He had a strong male demeanour, with what I would argue were good, communication skills. Mick engaged in open, unaggressive communication with all and sundry.

Mick was in tune with the environment and an expert in reptiles. He would just stop the car, jump out, and follow the tracks of large lace monitors and similar creatures into the sand dunes.

Eighty Mile Beach was very exposed. Five years prior, a cyclone had hit, denuding the foreshore of its vegetation. There were no mature trees and little shelter from the prevailing winds. My tent had taken a battering. I had to repair a snapped pole and add more guy ropes to support the windward side. In the midst, Mick wandered across and chatted a while. We agreed to throw a line in later in the day, when the tide was incoming and higher. The tides in that part of the world are enormous; Derby has the second highest rise and fall of tide in the world. At Eighty Mile Beach, the water receded over a kilometre at low tide.

That evening we headed a short distance from camp over the primary dune, with buckets, bait, fishing rods, and torch, to "wet a line." We had limited success. Mick caught a handful of assorted fish, mostly black-tipped sharks, which he had no time for. He released them back to the ocean. I had a few hits and managed to bring in a nice blue-nosed trout. It looked like a tailor, which I had caught years ago on Fraser Island, differing only by a blue tinge.

Later, back at the camp, I paneed the fillets and grilled the fish on my portable gas stove. I took some across to Mick, who was suitably impressed.

The next day, chatting with the locals, we were told that "the threadfin salmon were running," and there was a good fishing hole twelve kilometres up the beach. So that day we geared up for an attempt to fish off the beach and hook a salmon, the next morning. Mick was a seasoned fisherman, and he showed me how to rig the line. Mick showed me how to spread the line into three and twirl the outer two. Then he said, "Pick the middle one up with your teeth and pull it through. And you need a little bit of spit on it." It was something his grandfather had shown him as a boy, years prior.

Our rigs had three-gang hooks, a sinker with spikes that anchored in the sand against strong, surging tides. We used pilchards for bait. The weather was picture-perfect. Mick and I fished off that spot for the next week, the duration of our stay. We never missed catching some of those "big ones". The big ones were threadfin salmon and mulloway, ranging in weight from seven kilograms to ten and a half kilograms.

The fish came in to feed with the high tide and were caught in the gutter, approximately fifty metres off shore, in about two metres of water.

Sensationally, the line would rip: the reel zinged and literally squealed. The salmon would skim along the surface. At times they would swim toward the beach, create slack in the line, and try to spit the hook. On occasion they succeeded, and there are always the stories of those big ones that got away.

On the first day we kept one of the threadfin salmon for tucker by burying it in the damp sand and leaving only the tail protruding (another example of Mick's fishing know-how). The salmon supplied us with fresh fish for a week, and we released all others that we caught.

The locals were astonished that we let so many go. The locals were mainly retirees who had travelled north for the winter to bag their quota and then return home with a freezer full.

Mick caught many black-tipped sharks, a ray, and also a seagull that became entwined; all were set free.

A couple in their mid-fifties, tourists, Fritz and his wife, set up camp between Mick and me. It was just Mick's propensity to befriend the couple and spend time chatting in the evenings, in which I joined. Fritz was a novice fisherman, so Mick took him under his wing and invited him to come with us to the fishing hole the next day. Beforehand, Mick set up Fritz's tackle, and he was ready to go.

Under Mick's guidance, Fritz cast out and had his baited rig in the gutter with a chance to catch a big one. It was quite some time and many casts later when *crunch*! Fritz hooked a big one. I remember well his face of surprise and delight. Mick yelled instructions from a distance of twenty metres away: "Let her run. Keep the tension on, Fritz."

These threadfin salmon take fifteen to twenty minutes to reel in. They certainly fight. Mick, fearing Fritz would drop his first catch, waded into chest-deep water to grab the fish. Fritz was chuffed to have landed his first big one. It was congratulations and photos all round. It was a story that Fritz would tell time and time again, "The day fishing with Mick on Eighty Mile Beach, Western Australia, 2011."

Over our stay, Mick and I chatted about many incidents and things. On one particular evening, over a few beers and a shot or two of Mick's home-made grappa, I related my story to him of *Without Prejudice* and why I had decided to get out of the Queensland crab-pot. Mick said to me, and I believe from the conviction of his soul, "If that were me, I would be in jail."

There was no explanation needed for his would-be stance. However, by society's conditioned perception, and on face value of appearances, Mick would be labelled a big, bad bikie. Yet this was simply not the case. I found Mick to exhibit desirable human qualities of uncompromising conviction. He commented that by being in his organisation, he had learned respect of his fellow man, and it was the code he lived by. I believed, too, it was his heritage and Greek ancestry; filial piety is what the Buddhists understand it to be.

Mick was married with two grown children. He lived in the community as a well-balanced individual: husband, loving father, and now grandpa.

I have made the above statements regarding Mick's character to compare and contrast his demeanour with the demeanour of those with whom I have had dealings within the Queensland legal system. It is my observation that not one person in that system had proved to be worthy of my respect above Mick. Mick was a man of his word, in contrast to the solicitors and barristers I met who tended to disguise matters. Solicitors and barristers, as Sir Thomas Moore observed, use words to distort the truth, with no intention of keeping them. The lying, cheating words of the legal fraternity had been the bane of my existence for the last twenty-two years. These pundits, self-claimed pillars of society, can and do capriciously change or twist the meaning of words.

Mick to me was the epitome of what Jesus called "the salt of the earth." And it is known that salt adds flavour and preserves things.

The anointed ones live in ivory towers and believe they are above the law.

Mick and I broke camp at Eighty Mile Beach on the same day and arranged to catch up in Derby for some more fishing. One of the locals had given us the mail on barramundi at the head of the Fitzroy River.

We did a few early morning trips from the caravan park at Derby, about an hour and a half drive to the mouth of the Fitzroy River, chasing those elusive barramundi, but to no avail. On one particular trip down to the Fitzroy River, there were a group of Aboriginals milling around on the banks. As we approached near to their camp, where we were going to fish, Mick said to me out of the blue, "Don't be scared, 'cause I can fight." I cannot say if that was reassuring at the time. However, as things panned out, there was no confrontation, and we went about our fishing peaceably.

Mick told me how he had set off from Alice Springs in the Northern Territory, heading north. Just out of the Alice, he saw a sign that pointed left and said Kununurra, Western Australia. So, Mick turned left. The road he took from the left turn was the infamous Tanami Track. It treks the Tanami Desert for one thousand and four hundred unmade, gruelling kilometres: unrelenting gravel and dirt, with few fuel stops. He told me how he had pulled up the first night and made camp. About eleven o'clock that night, four adult male Aboriginals turned up and asked, "Do you have a hose?"

Mick was sitting at his campsite, whittling a branch with his hunting knife, and replied, "No, but I've got this two-litre empty bottle. If you want, you hold it and I'll cut the top off."

"No," said the enquirer.

"Why not?" asked Mick.

"Because I'm scared" was the answer.

After the visitors left, Mick tried to stay awake, sensing they would return, but he had driven most of the day and was exhausted. He inevitably fell asleep, around one or two o'clock in the morning.

Even though he purposely jack-knifed the trailer, as security, he surmised they returned and siphoned petrol from his tank. He woke next morning to find they had also taken his petrol cap. Mick was more so, most put out by that.

Mick was fortunate in that he had a long-range tank in his Jeep Cherokee. Yet he had barely enough fuel to get to the end of the fourteen-hundred-kilometre Tanami Desert Track, which meets the Great Northern Highway three hundred kilometres north of Kununurra.

We parted at Derby after a week. I departed a day early, as Mick had booked an appointment with the vet at Derby, to have his new pup immunised. The pup he named Derby Jack was purchased by donation to the Derby animal refuge, which had rescued the pup from cruelty and certain death.

I set off to do the Gibb River Road. Mick said, "After the fourteen hundred kilometres of gravel on the Tanami Desert Track, I've had enough dirt. I'm keeping to the bitumen."

The Gibb River Road was only half the distance of the Tanami Track and had just been opened by authorities that week, after being cut by the seasonal rains. The Durack River, the last major river crossing, had dropped to 0.7 metres, and that was considered the maximum depth of water to pass safely, by four-wheel drive vehicles only.

Having yet not seen Arnhem Land to compare, I found the Kimberley Region, which the Gibb River Road dissects, to be the most pristine country I had ever travelled. I was less than two hundred kilometres from the end of the dirt-gravel road when the Gibb River Road mauled my near-side rear tyre. The Kimberley Region is a remote, harsh arid environment: searing heat with little shade, corrugated roads with sharp rocks. But I managed to change the spare, get back to the bitumen, and proceed into Kununurra without further incident. There, I had the tyre replaced.

I too, decided that from then on there would be no more gravel roads or dirt tracks for me!

I continued southeast to Katherine, where I was told by the Aboriginal Land Council that access to Arnhem Land was unlikely until September because of the unprecedented wet season. Roads were still cut and under metres of water.

It was then I decided to return to Brisbane, to go back to challenge. I believed at the time I could somehow put the saga to bed and return to the Northern Territory to complete my trip to Arnhem Land later. A year later and it's still not an option to go back to the Northern Territory and tour Arnhem Land. I had sold my van after all the drama with the mechanic at the bottom of the Toowoomba Range and expense of the repair.

I exhausted my appeals for justice and again want out of the conundrum of Queensland governance and the cronyism of this unicameral state.

Mick, the bikie from Melbourne, and I keep in contact by infrequent email. We have agreement that there are no rules. But I would add, for the admonishment of those in their ivory towers and glass houses, that there is an exception to this rule, of 'no rules'. There is always an exception to every rule, and that for this rule, is that there is only one authority on earth.

CHAPTER 8

Ivory Towers and Glass Houses

Nearly twelve months to the day after I presented to Vladimir Rossi, MP, my submission to have my case tabled in the Australian Federal Parliament, to be examined by the Federal Executive Council Senate Committee, I had come to the end of the bumpy road. I had been off the beaten track, which turned out to be a dead-end road. The sojourn took twenty-two years to negotiate, only to arrive at a destination that was unforeseen, with the most undesirable outcome of no justice for my claim. My sojourn was now just a story.

Like the gravel tracks of the outback, I intend never to go there again.

It was the death of Steven R. that was the great leveller. It was a signpost saying, "Roads end. Turn around. The road is impassable."

I exhausted every avenue of appeal and had the realisation that life on earth is finite. I, like all the characters in my story, am not going to live forever. It was now time to move on and let past events go.

I have now planned to complete my story within the pages of this book because I believe the story needs to be told. There are no expected outcomes by having these books published. It merely serves me to have my story told; it fulfils my right to freedom of speech under our democratic constitution, a right which has been denied me by anointed ones. I am still resentful of being gagged and treated as a second-class citizen. I am appalled at the lack of spirit and compassion among those I have approached for help.

The model that persists is diametrically opposed to Albert Einstein's ideal. He stated, "I believe the most important mission of the state is to protect the individual and make it possible for him to develop into a creative personality."

I was outraged by the final response of the federal MP, Vladimir Rossi, and Senator Bill Gillard. For nine months they had me believing they were looking into my claim—taking action, doing something positive. Perhaps, by their authority, Rossi and Gillard could have considered pulling the indictments of Rathdowney from the state archives and forcing Rathdowney to comply with the conditions set forth in those indictments. Yet all along they were stalling, trying their best to wriggle out of what I regarded as an explosive situation. I was left hanging out to dry. Their total communication came in the form of a one-page letter from the senator, via the minister, to me.

The letter from Senator Bill Gillard, with the crown emblem on top, was addressed to Vladimir Rossi, MP, and read:

> I refer to your recent correspondence on behalf of your constituent, Mr Jan Gainsworthy, in respect of a legal matter he is involved in. I apologise for the delay in responding to you.
>
> I have read Mr Gainsworthy's correspondence carefully. I note his litigation commenced on the 11 June 2008 in the Brisbane District Court and the District Court judge struck out his Statement of Claim. I also note that Mr Jan Ernest Gainsworthy applied for leave to appeal to the Court of Appeal and that his application was refused on 27 October 2009. Mr Gainsworthy is now seeking to commence further proceedings against Rathdowney.
>
> Mr Jan Ernest Gainsworthy applied to the Queensland Public Interest Clearing House (PILCH) on 15 August 2011 for assistance with his litigation. I note QPILCH assessed his application and refused it on the grounds that it had limited prospects of success. Consequently, Mr Gainsworthy has written to you as

his Federal Member of Parliament, seeking further advice and assistance in this matter.

As this is a private legal matter, I am sure Mr Jan Ernest Gainsworthy can understand that the principal of independence of the courts prevent me, from commenting upon decisions handed down by the Brisbane District Court or the Court of Appeal.

Our system of democracy is built upon judicial independence and separation of powers. The courts are responsible for interpreting the law and deciding cases before it without Government interference, subject to any available review or appeal. Further, because Mr Jan Ernest Gainsworthy's complaint concerns the administration of State jurisdiction by the Queensland courts, there is no assistance I would be able to give from a federal perspective.

I appreciate that Mr Jan Ernest Gainsworthy is seeking assistance in his litigation; however, I am not in a position to provide him with legal advice. I can only advise that he seeks alternative legal representation. Mr Jan Ernest Gainsworthy should note that strict procedural rules and time limits apply in matters such as these and that at this late stage, unfortunately, his options appear very limited.

I trust this information is of assistance in responding to Mr Jan Ernest Gainsworthy

Yours faithfully

Senator William Archibald Gillard

I say, remonstrating in regard to Senator Bill Gillard's reply, "Bulldust, Billy-boy! You're a lying rodent!"

Einstein said of the truth, "It is difficult to say what truth is, but sometimes it is easy to recognize a falsehood."

I recognised instantly the falsehood. The gun barrister's reply was a whitewash and avoidance of his federal duties. I was not seeking litigation. I had asked for *help* and had the expectation that my submission would be tabled for a federal executive review to the Senate of the Australia Parliament. It was not for Billy-boy's jurisdiction, definitely, not for Senator Gillard's skewed and sole prejudicial judgement, coming nine months after my plea for help.

If my submission to parliament through the MP were so black and white, if neither could assist from the outset, then why did it take nine months to excuse themselves? You be the judge.

My submission was not put for a one-man decision. My affidavit was in the form of petition to the Federal Executive Council of the government of the day. The senator had *no* right to make a personal judgement and scuttle, by his non-action, my only hope of correcting a miscarriage of justice.

I would like to remind Senator Gillard of his inaugural parliamentary pledge: "For as long as I sit in this place I will defend the absolute right of all citizens to the free expression of their opinions, no matter how unfashionable, ignorant or offensive those opinions seem to others."

These are such hollow words now and illustrate the capriciousness of those who attain power and intend not to rock the boat. The senator is now in a glass house and cannot afford to throw stones because he would also be thrown from the ivory tower.

I was so angry with these two men, in that they had taken nine months to plot to cart me and my legal claim indefinitely. I imagine there must have been steam coming out of my ears. With a knee-jerk reaction, I began an acrid letter in reply.

(Jan Ernest Gainsworthy)

June 2012

Vladimir Rossi MP
Federal Member for Bonner
PO Box
Wynnum

Dear Sir

There are no words of gratitude contained in this letter.

Seldom do I retract my words, however, in this instance I make exception.

I take back the words of commendation I uttered initially in relation to you and Senator Gillard having integrity.

I was on my knees and your non-communication for nine months, together with the 'gun-barrister's insipid reply after nine months, has literally kicked the stuffing out of me.

I have barely the energy to write this reply, knowing that I am throwing darts at the stone-wall of the 'establishment'.

That is not to say I am giving up, but, on the contrary, I will dust myself off and doggedly press on.

You and Bill are now part of the contingent that has impeded the process of natural justice. I.e. you have covered up the truth and in effect have aided and abetted a criminal which has allowed a felon to go free.

Be it on your heads.

(This letter was never competed nor sent: I had given up on them.)

While I was suspended in time awaiting the senator's response, I again approached the Crime and Misconduct Commission, believing it was a crime or, at the very least, misconduct.

I asked directly why CMC did not follow up on what was stated three years before in their letter to me, dated April 2009. It said, "The CMC found, that the Legal Services Commission had a case to answer in regard to my initial complaint and the CMC would monitor the LSC investigation."

Once more I was fed hollow words, amounting to nothing of

substance. And too, there was never any follow-up by the CMC or reply from the LSC.

The QCMC, by sleight of hand, appointed a new case manager to my complaint, who conveniently knew nothing of my case. Therefore, he said he was "bound" not to act. A month and a half later, after my third approach to the CMC to enquire as to what course of action the CMC had embarked on regarding my concerns, the CMC responded with the following reply:

Dear Mr Jan Gainsworthy

RE: YOUR CONCERNS

Thank you for your further correspondence to the CMC dated May 2012 in which you reiterated your concerns in relation to your civil actions against S. Ruck and others, dating back to 2009.

You may recall that in our letter to you of June 2009 we explained our reasons for deciding not to take any action to this matter. Nothing that you have raised in your recent correspondence causes us to alter that earlier decision. As discussed with you previously, the CMC does not have jurisdiction over the conduct of private legal practitioners.

In relation to your concerns about further evidence coming to light, which was unavailable at the time of your appeal, you may wish to obtain independent legal advice in relation to any available legal options.

While we acknowledge that this matter remains of concerns to you, we are simply unable to assist you further.

Yours sincerely

Public Sector Program
Integrity Services

At this stage, Steven R. had passed, and I was resigned to the fact that it was over. I hastily sent the following one-page reply:

Jan Ernest Gainsworthy

July 2012

Public Sector Program
Integrity Services
Crime & Misconduct Commission
Brisbane

<u>Our Reference: MI-09-1367 MDK</u>

Dear Sirs

    Many thanks indeed for your recent correspondence, dated, June 2012.
    I am grateful for the CMC's deliberation and your definitive responses to my concerns. Again, thank you.
    Upon the CMC's findings and the advices proffered, I am forthwith dropping all pursuits regarding the matter.
    I accept fully that all that could be done has been done, and no further submissions to the CMC or any legal body will be necessary, nor forthcoming.
    It's over.
    I have closed my file and this chapter with the intention of moving on, to leave that past behind.
    All is well.

Yours sincerely

Jan Ernest Gainsworthy.

The Australian Federal Police responded similarly to the CMC by sending back to me all the material I had sent them, including a copy of *Without Prejudice*, saying that "it was not their jurisdiction and therefore they were unable to help."

It was the culmination of the nos of twenty-two years of struggling to be heard by the authorities I believed could help, would help me attain justice. The sudden death of Steven R. nailed the coffin shut.

That was it. It was well and truly time to capitulate. I was to wear the order of the courts, "That the writer had severely prejudiced the applicant / defendant, Joe Noel Rathdowney, and he (JNR) was unable to defend himself fairly because of the writer's delays." By their very order I was to pay Rathdowney's court costs and the court costs of his lying, cheating barrister, Cameron Douglas, SC, for his illegal submissions, which the DCJ, Betty Quincy, was so compelled to act on but not register.

I am exhausted, beleaguered, and despondent with my fellow man/woman.

Interestingly, no one has chased me for any outstanding fees. I think they are all fleeing their own indiscretions.

I had run the steeplechase of my life, and I believe I cleared every hurdle, yet there was never to be a first-prize blue ribbon. Not even an apology or a simple, "Sorry, Jan."

My only compassionate ally was my beloved aunt, God bless her. Aunt Evelyn, off her own bat, made an appointment with her local MP, Harold Jolly, in Melbourne to broach my justice claim and furnish him with a copy of my submission to the federal executive, along with a copy of my book, *Without Prejudice*. My understanding was that he, the Melbourne MP, lent a sympathetic ear, but had not the jurisdiction to act.

Evelyn approached in the same manner the MP for the Mallee, Frost, whom she knew in northern Victoria, and mailed the package to him. Frost replied by letter, saying he had spoken to Vlad Rossi, MP (presumably in Canberra), and the MP from Melbourne. Frost was to pass the copy of my book to Rossi, who would follow up.

I thought it fascinating that my MP Rossi, had now a copy of my book. However, Vladimir Rossi, MP's follow-up was to get with Senator Gillard and hatch a plan to dump me, who was a niggling thorn in their sides.

I had also, while on hold, written to another independent senator with a legal background, Senator Xavier Nixon, seeking advice. I too had posted the independent senator a copy of my newly published book, *Without Prejudice*.

After Steven R.'s death, I hastened to send Senator Nixon a letter requesting he destroy the file and to ignore my earlier request to petition the senate.

As with all other members of parliament and senators whom I had approached, there was a deadly silence and no response whatsoever.

This was my closing letter to the independent senator:

Jan Ernest Gainsworthy

Senator Nixon

    I have recently had responses to my legal concerns from the Australian Federal Police and the Crime and Misconduct Commission and both have indicated that nothing further can be done.

    Upon their advices and the sudden death of a good friend I have decided to cease and desist, any further action in regard to my legal pursuits to get closure for my saga.

    The ordeal has been adverse to my mental and physical states of health and I am not willing to subject myself to further stresses.

    In that regard, my instruction to you is to now not file my petition (submission) in Parliament.

    I truly regret any inconvenience that may have been caused by my initial correspondence.

    I now respectfully request that you destroy the file and consider it 'water under the bridge'; that which I intend to do.

    I apologise too, if in the first instance you were placed in an awkward position, due to my bloody mindedness. Sorry.

    The saga now, after 20 odd years is just a story and I

shall close the chapter and complete the ending. It's not quite how I had anticipated, but it's finished.

I now accept that one individual cannot change the course of the system. I have done all that was possible; sought every avenue that was available to me and I have simply exhausted every option and have chosen to turn my back and walk away before the matter consumes me totally by ill health.

There are far more serious injustices in the World, than that I have had to endure.

The matter now is to me no more than a storm in a tea-cup, just a story of the past to be told in the sequel to "Without Prejudice." The sequel is to be titled simply "Justice" and subtitled, "A Well Guarded Open Secret."

Again, many thanks indeed for your considerations.

I wish you well with your platform of poker machine reform.

All is well.
Kind regards
Yours sincerely

Jan Ernest Gainsworthy

The silver-lining to this very dark cloud was that there were no more letters to write, no more graveyard shifts suspended in time, waiting for the tinkling of the bell to indicate there was life in the corpse of my justice pursuit.

There was not even the option of having the question put to the condemned, "One for the road or are you staying on the wagon?"

The brutal truth was that the saga was dead and buried. It was now just a story printed on the pages of this book. And as to what's next and where to now? It is anybody's guess. I say, "GOK: God only knows."

However, I am sure I will be far from the madding crowd and any court, especially in Queensland. I believe for the anointed ones, they have had a pyrrhic victory too. Their karma is sure to follow, but I hasten to add, "Instant coffee is not quick enough."

So be it on their heads.

There is only one authority on earth.

CHAPTER 9

The Brutal Truth and My Disclaimer

I now believe there is nothing more to say and accept nothing more can be done physically, in the material world. However, I do lament over the ghastly outcome of having investment funds embezzled and years of prime life stolen by the denials of the anointed ones.

My belief in a just legal system has been razed to the ground.

The Buddhists believe you must go to ground zero before you can go anywhere. Well, I have arrived. This is a phrase I plagiarized from my good friend Sami. "Doing the dream Gainsworthy", she would riposte.

I can imagine that the rats with the gold teeth are crowing now, "We told you so, Jan."

I, also imagine, too, that those anointed ones will be a little displeased that their satanic works are documented in the body of my books. They have stymied me and gagged me from airing this story, yet they are unable to make a law to suppress true freedom of speech. That is a brutal truth for the anointed ones.

My court hearings are now on public record. What I have put in the pages of my books is now public property for anyone who may wish to access the material and read. For the most part, my chores are done. We cannot undo the past, but we can reflect and avoid similar mistakes in the future.

That said, it would take courage and conviction of the individual, which is another brutal truth to address.

The indiscretions dealt me by the system were of man's clever, restrictive thinking. Short-sightedness and sleight-of-hand tactics are used to veil the frailty of what is, to me, a corrupted system, devoid of the golden rule.

Integrity and ethics have been usurped by greed, the love of money.

Power and image have replaced fairness and the right of individual expression. As a worldly example, I allude to David Gillespie's findings on sugar, or the fructose component of sugar, as "a major public health risk."

Gillespie, an attorney, published his findings in his book, *Sweet Poison: Why Sugar Makes Us Fat*. Gillespie boldly states his claim that sugar is a major health issue, supported by facts and scientific argument. Yet, as he states, "The authorities were unwilling to heed my findings because there is simply too much money involved." The irony for me here is that David Gillespie is an attorney, an anointed one.

My concern is, what legacy are we as a society cementing for our future generations? At stake are the health issues of obesity and the epidemic lifestyle disease of type-two diabetes, which sugar contributes to due to its overuse in our processed foods.

I have this, my story of injustice, as a legacy to tell to my grandchildren. And what story do the anointed ones tell their grandchildren to justify their lofty positions of office, their accumulated wealth, and their denial of truth, such as in my case?

I surmise that the anointed ones' story would go like this in regards to my case: "It was only one person, Jan. He was crying over spilled milk. Jan wasn't even a solicitor nor versed in law! Justice was seen to be done; Jan Gainsworthy had his day in court. We, the law fraternity gods, cannot allow an outsider such as Jan Ernest Gainsworthy to interpret our written rules and spill the open secret that our cult is not entirely squeaky clean and above the law. Who does Jan Gainsworthy think he is?"

The word will be on the street now that I have capitulated.

I can see an angry response to this second book, *Those in Ivory Towers: Lawmakers Lawbreakers*, when it is published. The content clearly illustrates the closing of the ranks by authorities, now having to protect an absurd court ruling; to what Lord Diplock may say of the decision: "So outrageous in its defence of logic or accepted moral standards that no sensible person who had applied his mind to the question to be decided could have arrived at it."

At this point now, I will qualify my verbosity against the anointed ones. It is my disclaimer, the fine print. I have in the main belittled all the legal profession and politicians. There are honourable people within the system, and it is unreasonable to throw a blanket over all of them. I direct my comments only to those I have had direct dealings with. Yet, these individuals I make comment of have tarnished the public perception of the system further. For everybody, a decree: "If the cap fits, wear it."

Surely, if any of the players read this book, they will be totally embarrassed. Then again, maybe those doing the Devil's work would not be; the Devil doesn't do shame or guilt, apparently. The brutal truth is they have plundered and perjured themselves for the sake of one crooked lawyer. Their actions cannot be undone unless there is admission of error at law, and that simply will not happen. It would take courage to break ranks within their glass house.

The judge of the Supreme Court, Brisbane, presiding over the case:

Kevin Joana (Clive Kerry Fletcher), Keat-Wyatt and Associates, and Ors V Dundas (the retired farmer, Henry Wilfred Dundas) interestingly, and unconnectedly, His Honour, quoted another finding of Lord Diplock.

His Honour said of Lord Diplock's observations in a judgement of the Privy Council:

> Although in the normal way it is not appropriate for a judge to attempt to resolve conflicts of evidence on affidavit, this does not mean that he is bound to accept uncritically, as raising a dispute of fact which calls for further investigation, every statement of an affidavit however equivocal, lacking in precision, inconsistent with undisputed contemporary documents or other statements by the same deponent, or inherently improbable in itself it may be.

These observations were applied to Fletcher's (Kevin Joana) belated assertion of a five-year agreement between Henry Dundas and himself.

It was an out-and-out lie put forward by Fletcher's solicitor, Joe Noel Rathdowney, of Rathdowney MacDraw, and defence counsel, Cameron Douglas, SC, with Paul Black.

Seen it all before? J. N. Rathdowney has tainted the Queensland legal system by his litany of lies and outrageous, underhanded tactics to silence my claim. It is a foul stench.

But look, look at all the "Ors" Rathdowney has dragged into his crab-pot. All those privileged anointed ones who are seemingly quite prepared to climb into the pot and put up with the odour and have their robes stained, as he.

Perhaps, in the future, they will decree a new code of dress for the cult, that being the addition of mandatory gas masks to go with their black robes, which cover up those stains. Perhaps, just perhaps, they will dye their wigs and add a little glitter to enliven their disguise. All at the taxpayers' expense, of course!

The guarding of the open secret also serves to show how very few take on law as a profession with the intention of seeing justice carried out in society, and how very few anointed ones who enter politics have any regard for their constituents above the power, position, and remuneration.

Oh, how too are they so quick to seek absolution? Quick to find someone to blame and make an example of, to excuse themselves for their own sins. The case in point I make mention of is the treatment of Donald Norton by the Queensland government. To me, the treatment of Norton was unconstitutional, grossly overt, and shameful conduct by the Queensland Parliament to mock and scorn the man's plea for mercy.

From Daniel Hurst's article, 13 May 2011, in the *Brisbane Times*, titled "MPs Deride Norton's Plea for Mercy," Hurst reported Norton saying, "Capone did less time than me."

During his speech, Norton said he struggled every day to understand how a "loan" arrangement with the late businessman Keith Torbec was criminal.

Norton was the first prisoner in Queensland's history to address the legislative assembly. He began by making reference to himself as Daniel in the Scriptures, who survived being placed in a den of lions. Donald Norton reflected on the Roman Empire and how in those times, Christians were fed to the lions at the Colosseum.

Norton called for a judicial inquiry into the QCMC and the office of the Department of Public Prosecutions.

Hurst reported that the speech, before a packed media and public gallery, ended at 12:36 p.m., nine minutes short of the time allotted for him.

With sombre mood in the air, Norton ended his speech by urging MPs to read Matthew 7: 1-2.

"May God bless you all and keep you safe from harm," Donald Norton said in conclusion.

According to the article, there was one independent MP, Lachlan McAvoy, who visited Norton in jail. McAvoy defended the former minister, saying he appeared to be an intelligent man and keenly aware of democratic conventions.

"I'm sorry, I didn't see the monster that some of the members of this House want to see," Mr McAvoy said.

My critique of the article is that the reporter too was biased and had prejudged Donald Norton. He sided with the skewed prejudgement of the Queensland Parliament.

I believe Donald is no saint. But he has served his time and should be released from jail, as he is no threat to the community.

I empathise with Donald Norton. I can see glaring similarities of how the one house of the Queensland Parliament unjustly and unconstitutionally stitched up a good man and disallowed him natural justice. Donald Norton was set up to be thrown to the lions of the shonky Queensland Parliament. The numbers, stacked, furthered a biased and prejudged outcome.

Donald Norton was used by the MPs as a scapegoat, someone to lay the blame on and wipe the blood off their hands from all their past, shady deals and indiscretions. This was a show of power and a facade of righteousness, thinly veiled and disguised thuggery to portray integrity.

Donald admonished the MPs, citing the gospel of Matthew, chapter 7, verses 1 and 2, which read:

> Do not judge and criticize and condemn others, so that you may not be judged and criticized and condemned yourselves.
>
> For just as you judge and criticize and condemn others you will be judged and criticized and condemned,

and in accordance in the measure you deal out to others it will be dealt out again to you. [Online NIV]

This is the wheel of fortune I alluded to in chapter 2.

Those who have falsely testified against Donald Norton or have said nothing in his defence will, in the Lord's time, have the karma of what goes around, comes around, to personally deal with.

The one house of the Queensland Parliament is the epitome of a den of thieves: a pit and brood of vipers, controlled by one individual who can censure the whole of the parliament.

Unicameralism has in the state of Queensland denied its constituents of true democracy, individual rights, and natural justice, and has stripped the public of a functioning constitutional agenda.

The individual power of the premiers has robbed not just me and Donald, but society of a transparent justice system.

Fairness, equity, and the right to be heard is devoid in this rogue state, and alarmingly, I see the trend oozing into the federal arena, dripping from the anointed ones who were tarred with the brush in Queensland.

The Queenslanders have managed to attain high-ranking positions of the Australian Parliament and also the High Court of Australia, which may be seen as politically appointed positions.

A most recent controversial example is the appointment by the premier, Neville Chamberlin, of Judge Tom McCardle from the district court to Chief Justice of the Supreme Court of Queensland. Tom Carmody was the commissioner of the Hinze Affair, mentioned in chapter 6, he would have first-hand knowledge of injustice, cover-up and the players. That is not within the intended scope of this book, but I make mention of the point because I am sure political appointments have been a contributing influence in my overwhelming struggle to be heard, even at the federal level.

On their heads, be it.

The wheel turns, and the brutal truth does not go away. Truth cannot be buried forever. There are no secrets. One can deny the truth, but that does not change the truth. You cannot go around, up, under, or over the truth as an obstacle; you must go through.

The brutal truth from my perspective: there is only one authority on earth.

Albert Einstein eloquently stated, "Whoever is careless with the truth in small matters cannot be trusted in important affairs."

CHAPTER 10

Savagery, Sleight of Hand, and Silence

Savagery, sleight of hand, and silence are depicted by me as the modus operandi of the cloistered Queensland legal and political system. These three Ss conjured by the one-house state, have seemingly seeped into the federal arena.

"Politics is a pendulum whose swings between anarchy and tyranny are fuelled by perennial rejuvenated illusions," said Albert Einstein. And further, Einstein was quoted as saying, "Without 'Ethical Culture', there is no salvation for humanity."

Donald Norton, at the hands of these thugs, has shone through, kept the faith, and illustrated how rules are contorted to paint a squeaky-clean image of politicians and the administration of justice for the masses, which complacently swallow the government's plethora of lies and manufactured illusions.

Norton, nailed the standard, when he urged MPs to read Matthew 7:1–2.

I would go further and say to the MPs, "Don't only read the verses but act upon the advice given, because the Bible is the manufacturer's instruction and service manual."

If something goes wrong with the car, we take it to a mechanic or look it up in the service manual for a remedy.

The wheels of the legal and political system have fallen off and are in dire need of repair. Those in the driving seat are not prepared to give up their power and get out and change a tyre, for fear of loss of credibility. They lack faith and trust no one. They know naught of the one authority.

My experience was that I was victim to sleight of hand in the district court, savagery in the Queensland Supreme Court of Appeal, and silence dealt me in the High Court of Australia. I didn't even hear the sound of the pen putting a line through my affidavit of appeal to the High Court of Australia.

I have compared and contrasted Donald's account with mine, and I believe they were similar, although the savagery dealt Norton was far in excess of my mild form. My experiences would validate Donald Norton's allegations that the QCMC picks and chooses at its whim: "It picks and chooses according to its own agenda," Donald said. And Donald alleged that the office of the Director of Public Prosecutions turned a blind eye too, accusing the CMC of pursuing him as "revenge" and claiming the DPP's office had improperly interfered in one of his trials.

I heard on the grapevine that the Queensland Treasury was approached by the DPP for funds to go after Norton; the unsubstantiated reply was from the normally tight-fisted department was, "How much do you need? You can have as much as you like to nail him."

From that biased approach, Norton never stood a chance. The public purse was opened wide to get the contrived result and a conviction with stacked evidence for the benefit of political appointments. The anointed ones had their scapegoat and could shift the blame to Norton, conveniently all funded by public moneys.

I, like the independent minister of parliament, Lachlan McAvoy, cannot see the monster in Norton as the Office of the Public Prosecutions contrived.

I cringed at the slurs made by the speaker of the house, the premier, and the MPs on the day Donald Norton's plea for mercy was put before the Queensland legislative assembly.

This was a gig for sure, set up by the premier and Queensland Parliament.

It was a sham. Queensland has not had a senate since 1921, in which the legislative assembly is normally embodied. How then could the premier call Donald Norton before the legislative assembly if, clearly, the legislative assembly does not exist? This was a well-planned manoeuvre to garner public support for ridding the Queensland Parliament of all corruption and to project a false image of innocence and uprightness.

Contrary to the constitution and conventions of natural justice, Donald Norton was dragged into the chamber and put into stocks for public embarrassment. The gallery threw muck at him, condemned before he opened his mouth.

Norton's words just bounced off the blocked ears and stonewall of the anointed gallery. Those waiting for Norton to finish would, without deliberation, bring down their contrived, contorted retribution in the form of a prejudiced finding.

A bogus finding too, manipulated by those in the ivory tower of Queensland government. An unconscionable act of aggression toward a man on his knees, pleading for mercy. All Queenslanders condoning such a barbaric act should be ashamed of the injustice dished up to Donald Norton. Without Prejudice, indeed! And, as Norton had pointed out, he received a harsher sentence than Al Capone.

However, Donald Norton can stand tall for his resilience and strength of character, demonstrated by the calm of his closing words:

> Today all of us have the opportunity to cease and forgive.
>
> I'm bloodied but not broken. I have fought the good fight and have finished the race and I have kept the faith.
>
> May God bless you all and keep you safe from harm.

What I think Donald was saying, ever so succinctly, is: "The wheel turns; what goes around comes around. This world is ephemeral. There is only one authority on earth, and one of its most basic rules, cause and effect, is prescribed in Matthew 7:1–2. Read it!"

My research has led to another fascinating insight into the corruption in the Australian government, judiciary, and federal police.

The book that reveals all is written and self-published by author Kane Denver. *Love Letters from the Bar Table* is the book's title. I was initially grabbed by the title; you just have to love it. Quoting from the website:

> Some of the topics of the book raises and/or deals with are: judicial bias – judicial corruption - bribes – perceived bias – actual bias – breaching the Barristers Rules - the breaching of Solicitor Rules – lack of ethics – abusing procedural fairness – abuse of processes – delaying tactics – over-charging – attempted fraud – criminal conduct – attempting to pervert the course of justice – fabricating evidence – dereliction of duty – shredding of evidence, a personal interest to Kane.

Wow! Well, that about sums it up, ay? There are a few things there that the rats won't do, but everything on the list is taken up by the legal system, so the rats don't have to worry.

I think Mr Denver may have missed the deployment of silence, or what I would term "the Fifth Amendment," applied liberally on Australian soil.

Silence goes hand in hand with non-action. The anointed ones have mastered the art of sitting on their hands and staying silent. The exception to this guarded open secret is if, and only if, there are political points to score.

Kane Denver has also set up a blog, called the "Kangaroo Court" website.

There is also an online shop that sells T-shirts with demeaning slogans regarding solicitors and judges.

Transcribed below is the review of Kane Denver's book, *Love Letters from the Bar Table*, by an English barrister, Taylor Swift, MBE, of Richmond Grey Chambers:

> I'm always interested in a cross-section of law books depicting the working of common law across its jurisdictions. When I came across this curious self-published work, 'Love Letters from the Bar Table', from Shane Dowling, who has a certain number of 'issues' with the legal establishment in Australia, I thought it was worth looking at further.
>
> A doctrine which is gaining international popularity at present is called 'judicial recusal' where a judge stands aside (or is made to stand aside) in certain circumstances

based on the two main rules of natural justice, namely; a judge may not act in his own cause; and both sides must be heard. New Zealand academic, Grant Hammond, has written a definitive work on the current state of the law.

I think it's a fair comment to say we do not have any recognised corruption within the judiciary in the United Kingdom. I, for one, have grave reservations about the strength of any argument suggesting forms of corruption elsewhere amongst judges because of the catastrophic constitutional implications involved.

So, what I am saying here is I have no idea of the rights and wrongs of Kane Denver's detailed case. I don't offer an opinion although I have read his documents and his views in his book in some detail. What I do say, however, is I feel the worth of the book merits some consideration in relation to the basic concepts we hold true in common law tradition, namely upholding rules of natural justice.

The book is described as a true story about the systematic scandalization of the Australian Federal Judicial System; In 18 chapters and just over 300 pages, a case is being made out that certain people are, by definition, 'corrupt' and 'taking bribes'. But it is one-sided and silence and in action on the other.

The problem remains that where judicial decisions are made and one party becomes aggrieved by the outcome, the phrase 'sour grapes' springs to mind.

I feel Denver doesn't suffer from sour grapes but the other perennial, 'being ignored'.

It is only relatively recent in the UK that judges now give interviews or sometimes reply to correspondence (through their clerks) so I'm not surprised by the tactics employed in the 'stop (or rather ignore) Denver's campaign. Frankly, I doubt he will ever get closure on his matter, but he raises a most important principle – that is; 'When should a judge retire from a hearing', or, 'when can we question a judge?'

I came away from this book with very perplexed feelings. Mr R. Kramer will do nothing; the Australian judiciary would never acknowledge any form of corruption as I see it; and the case for a Royal Commission (or whatever name you want to call it in the future) is many years away, if ever it is convened, and gives any form of realistic appraisal to be acted upon. So, what to do?

Well, Denver has raised the consciousness of the issue in parallel with increases in judicial recusal applications as the wider public become more aware of the failings of judges. Frankly, it's a can of worms with no winners on the horizon here.

But I would like to think that the ironically named, 'Love Letters from the Bar Table' is a marker setting a future agenda for international human rights and upholding the rules of natural justice in the tradition of a discussion on a new 'Table Talk" theme- It's a valuable contribution to the debate of about how we face the future in the global discussion age of the internet ... and where judges (and politicians) will have to face up to a new agenda of jurisprudential responsibility by answering their critics if our accepted concept of natural justice is ignored.

Reading

The above insert is a quiz. What does it mean?

Answer: Reading between the lines.

I see the reviewer is a pompous ol' pommy who denies any "recognised corruption within the judiciary in the United Kingdom."

My first reaction was, how short-sighted and prudish can one English barrister be? Does Swift think the English rid themselves of corruption two-hundred and thirty years ago by shipping the convicts out to Australia and setting up the ten-pound tourist scheme?

Aside from my digression and cheap shot, Swift made some pertinent observations and salient statements regarding the "future agenda for international human rights," together with "the two main rules of natural justice," namely, "a judge may not act in his own cause; and both sides must be heard."

I concur with Taylor that the "the global discussion age of the internet" will eventually uncover the buried, well-guarded, open secret of our politicians and legal fraternity.

It appears nobody from within is willing to acknowledge the need for change at this stage. There is insufficient critical mass from the outside to blow the lid off the iniquitous, self-serving political and legal systems.

Maybe it will take a generation to say, "Enough is enough!" However, that, as I have said, will take courage and conviction. The masses need to comprehend that there is only one authority on earth, but that lesson is shielded by our educational system, which has perpetuated that madness from day dot, especially in the state of Queensland.

I had yet another epiphany. The reason those of the Queensland legal and political systems are a little behind in thinking resources is because they have been "educated," or conditioned, by the very system they uphold. That insight by me is still pertinent in 2018. The system was fabricated by those snatching control in the early days; so very limiting and subversive toward its people is Queensland governance.

My perception of the bumbling, restrictive governance of Queensland finds me seething. They know there is naught an outsider can do which would influence the anointed ones to overturn a judge's decision. My last hoorah was jettisoned by what I term the Queensland connection, which has permeated the federal parliament of Australia and the Australian High Court, Canberra.

CHAPTER 11

From Pillar to Post:
The Last Hoorah

After returning to Nitmiluk Gorge from the far north-west, I was told by the Aboriginal Land Council that access to Arnhem Land was unlikely until September because of the unprecedented wet season; roads were still cut and impassable. It was then I decided to return to Brisbane, to go "back to challenge." I believed at that time I could somehow put the saga to bed and return to the Northern Territory to complete my trip to Annie's Land within three months.

Returning to Brisbane, initially I had no idea where to start. But, I had inkling to check for priors and for a pattern to Rathdowney's systematic steps to defraud me and Ors and to then cover up, with the protection of a few individuals in the Queensland legal fraternity.

What the legal system of Queensland had not reckoned on was the new age: the power of the computer and ready access to public records made available by the laws of freedom of information that now exist.

This freedom of information now exists as a right to information (RTI). It is a landmark, a restriction lifted by people power and their claiming of rights for individuals.

It is also an erosion of the anointed ones' power. No longer can they bury information and make it inaccessible to the public. Yet, somehow, Rathdowney managed to conceal two indictments in the Queensland state archives for sixty-five years and had a crucial court file destroyed without being archived after twelve years.

Prior to the year 2000, the general public—the person on the street, such as I am—had difficulty in researching files, attaining the acts and the Uniform Civil Procedure rules, and viewing the orders put down by Their Honours. The computer age, as Taylor Swift described, together with the right to information, has changed all that.

Presently, "in the global discussion age of the internet ... judges (and politicians) will have to face up to a new agenda of jurisprudential responsibility by answering their critics if our accepted concept of natural justice is ignored." [Book preview, *Love Letters from the Bar Table*, by Taylor Swift]

The information gleaned by searching files on the net was a revelation. I even searched my own name on Queensland e-court files and came up with the files of the district court and the Brisbane Supreme Court of Appeal. That is how I know my hearing was to be set down in chambers. That fact still exists on Queensland e-court summary files today!

The Australian High Court has a separate website for their files.

From other files retrieved from the district court and the Supreme Court Brisbane Registry of Rathdowney and Ruck, I compiled two separate dossiers, one on Joe Rathdowney and the other on Sean Ruck. All the information is freely available on the public record; however, I am continuing with the theme of assumed names. My intention is not to name individuals because it would breach the rules of parliamentary privilege, as I believed my affidavit with submissions was to be tabled in the senate for the federal executive to consider. The following two dossiers were to be tabled, which were part of my indexed, paginated bundle of evidence.

JNR Deceit

Rathdowney's Path of Deceit

The following is an expose` of J.N. Rathdowney's deceit as a solicitor within the Queensland Legal System.

I, Jan Ernest Gainsworthy, was a client of Rathdowney MacDraw and Joe Rathdowney receipted moneys placed into their Trust Account in 1990.

The Firm have STILL not accounted for these funds; 25/8/2011.

Rathdowney has denied I was a client of his. This is contempt and the QLS and the Courts of Queensland should hold him accountable for such an untruth.

QLS and the Courts of Queensland have accepted Rathdowney's word on face value that the funds were for a client, Kevin Joana. (Clive Fletcher)

It was not until 2008 that the TRUTH was unearthed. Eighteen years concealed and held by the QLS.

From exhibits of Rathdowney's Application to have our case thrown out; reveals the Trust Ledger, Diary Notes and QLS documentation plainly showing the contortions of the legal processes, twisted, to cover up this fraud.

A company, Keat-Wyatt & Associates, elucidated from the Trust Ledger was paid $112,000.00 over a period of two years.

The Director of the Company was Kevin Joana / Clive Fletcher. Further investigation revealed that Polteka P/L was a Holding Company of Keat-Wyatt & Associates and from ASIC Records it can be stated as fact that Joe Rathdowney was an Associate Director of Polteka P/L; binding Rathdowney as a business partner to Kevin Joana. (Clive Kerry Fletcher); not merely a client as JNR falsely stated.

From the very out-set Rathdowney & Joana were business partners and had put together the now failed "TOBJOANO" over-seas' funding scam.

It is on record that Fletcher, (Joana) & Rathdowney were brought before the District Court for "money owing" File No. PLT603/92; The Pineapple Pastoral Co.PL – V- C.K.F. Finance PTY LTD.

Keat-Wyatt & Associates was stated as being the 'consulting arm' of - C.K.F. Finance PTY LTD. (Clive Kerry Fletcher/Kevin Joana).

In another case file; Devine –V- Rathdowney

& Anor; File No. PLT1315/93 Joe Rathdowney was Defendant of a claim of damages. There are no further details because this file has been destroyed by the court's administration before being archived.

Further, there have been three separate complaints about Rathdowney regarding "money owing," to the Queensland Law Society. The Parties complaining were; Jan Ernest Gainsworthy; Beounce' and De-Silver, the QLS ignored all three claims although Rathdowney was charge criminally TWICE in 1992-1993.

As recently as May 2009 Fletcher, Keat-Wyatt & Associates and another Company, ACACIA RIDGE DEVELOPMENTS PTY LTD were brought before the Supreme Court of Queensland for, you guessed it,

'**Moneys Owing**' of the magnitude of $2.7 million dollars.

Rathdowney (demonstrated sheer contempt and abuse of court process) along with counsel, Cameron Douglas SC & P. Black, who represented the defendants, knowingly that they, the defence lawyers, had vested interest in the out-come.

FILE No. 12147 of 2008

Joe Rathdowney was an Associate Director of Polteka P/L that is listed on ASIC Records as being a former registered Office of ACACIA RIDGE DEVELOPMENTS PTY LTD.

On the second Citation, 11 December 2009, another Company linked to Kevin Joana, (Fletcher), Keat-Wyatt & Associates and another Company, ACACIA RIDGE DEVELOPMENTS PTY LTD, and Polteka P/L was Piamo pastoral Pty Ltd. A search of ASIC Records shows a former Registered Office of Piamo pastoral Pty Ltd., to be RATHDOWNEY & MacDraw SOLICITORS, LEVEL 2 LJHOOKER HOUSE ACACIA RIDGE QLD.

This startling fact revealed that Joana (Clive Fletcher) and Keat-Wyatt & Associates, faced the Court for "moneys owing," also directly implicates J.

N. Rathdowney in embezzling $2.7 million dollars of Dundas' funds. Order: 11/01/2009 FILE No. Supreme Court of Queensland: BS 12147 of 2008.

Further too; it is on Public record in the Queensland State Achieves that Joe Noel Rathdowney was severed with two indictments; Item ID Nos.; 1227093 & 1227094. 1992/3

I had in July 1993 made official complaint to Sergeant Lance Michaels of Brisbane CIB and recorded the same complaint at my local CIB.

Rathdowney in 1993 was indicted on two occasions and I believe having been indicted should have been stripped of his licence to act as a solicitor, in the interest of Public security.

Henry Wilfred Dundas could well have been protected from the embezzlement of Clive Fletcher (Kevin Joana) and his partner Joe Rathdowney.

Jan Ernest Gainsworthy

24 August 2011

"Priors of Ruck"

The following is a recently gleaned expose` of Sean J. Ruck, solicitor, whom the writer took into his confidence and trusted, as he (Ruck) was a practising solicitor of the Queensland Supreme Court, and he showed a personal and particular interest in my case.

My bitter experience with Ruck has in the writer's opinion proven him to be a "bully" and a person of little substance, driven by greed and the power of money.

By his very actions, Sean Ruck has demonstrated unconscionable professional behaviour in manipulating the Court processes for the benefit of him, ruthlessly despatching individuals, regardless of their legal correctness.

It is on Record that Ruck was a respondent to a claim of the Appellants' that he was implicated in unjust process of the Court, and colluded with the Appellant's solicitor, Sandy, to arrange a consented agreement at the Hearing.

The Appellants' Exhibit 'A' of their Affidavit; File No. 7 of 1998, Queensland Supreme Court, Black Rock, is a hand scrawled agreement written on a Ruck's letter head with the details also of Jerry Abbott. Clearly, there was neither negotiation nor review by His Honour, Baden-Clay. 15/3/1998. Taken directly as an excerpt from the Transcripts of Proceedings, His Honour Baden-Clay stated he did not wish to, "accede" Jerry Abbott of Counsel for Rupert Axtell, Ruck's client.

The Second Appeal was to the Supreme Court Brisbane, Court of Appeal No. 8032 of 1998. President Mahoney Dismissed leave to Appeal with costs, (26/43000), as Their Honours did with the writer. The Appellants were denied natural Justice and an opportunity to be heard, biased by Ruck & Abbott.

One Appellant succumb to cancer about two years ago, however, I contend that her ill-treatment by Sean Ruck, Jerry Abbott, and the Queensland Legal system would have contributed greatly to her demise.

The Appellants of the two Appeals were Defendants in a personal injury case of Rupert Axtell; Supreme Court Queensland, Black Rock Registry; File No. 26 of 1995.

Axtell engaged Ruck to falsely accuse the Defendants and hold them accountable for injuries Axtell sustained, brought about by Rupert himself.

From the Defendants' Affidavit, accessed by the writer at the Black Rock, Supreme Court Registry; the defendants under oath told the Court they were never Rupert Axtell's employer and described Axtell as a squatter, having lived in a house on their property and never having paid rent.

The Court, with Justice Baden-Clay presiding, ignored Appellants' defence that Rupert Axtell pestered appellants to "borrow" the post-hole auger which subsequently Axtell injured himself with.

Again, they were denied natural justice.

Had the writer known Ruck was capable of such immoral, outrageous conduct I would have never engaged him as my Solicitor in any form of representation.

Ruck has also been brought before the Court as Defendant by the Deputy Commissioner of Taxation for 'Moneys Owing'; District Court File No. PLT2935/92

This expose` underpins my NOW character opinion of Sean J. Ruck as being 'shady' and not a person fit to hold Office as a solicitor of the Supreme Court in Queensland.

From my experiences Ruck has brought disrepute to the legal profession and tarnished the Public perception of the whole of the Queensland Legal System.

Having the priors of Ruck elucidated I am now confident that he, Ruck, can be held accountable for non-specific performance by not executing his duties in a timely manner and failing to have my Claim upheld and my funds placed in Rathdowney MacDraw's Trust recovered.

Having gleaned this recent findings of Ruck's past actions I contend that Ruck's systematic steps in handling my case were for his own monetary ends and had an agenda, colluded with Rathdowney, to interfere with Court processes and have my legitimate Claim thrown out on a false precept of "Laches" or delays on the writer's part.

I am aggrieved and seek restitution for his unconscionable conduct as an Officer of the Court.

Jan Ernest Gainsworthy

I wholly believe if I had paid Ruck $5,000 to represent me on the day of the district court, the hearing would have taken place in the chambers—not an open court, as it was—without witnesses or Rathdowney's counsel, Cameron Douglas, SC.

Ruck would have scuttled our claim and allowed Rathdowney's application to be upheld, as was the case, but with no input from myself nor any legal defence from Sean Ruck. I contend that no one else except Ruck, Rathdowney, and the judge would have known what went down behind the closed doors of the scheduled chamber hearing. It would have been the death of our claim there and then, buried in the court's registry and even, maybe, destroyed, just to be sure.

My court appearance was a spanner in the work. It set Ruck off; he was seething with anger and embarrassment that he had been caught out fiddling the system by an outsider, me.

What Sean Ruck had set in place blew up in his face. Now, what was Ruck going to tell Joe Rathdowney about their plan imploding?

It was 4:32 p.m. on the day before the chamber hearing. I also believe part of the persistence of Ruck, in demanding that I pay an extra $5,000 upfront to represent me on the day, was a strategy to have me pull out. Again, that would have left Rathdowney's application to be upheld because no one would front the court. And the judge would have stricken out our statement of claim in accordance the Uniform Civil Procedure rules, with never any avenue of appeal.

Ruck and Rathdowney would have been well aware of that outcome, and in their conniving would have anticipated that was the way the chips would fall for Jan Ernest Gainsworthy. They too would have been alive to the fact that the other two plaintiffs, Henry Tingay and Wayne Peterman, would drop the claim if I, Jan, was eliminated by their underhanded, collaborative scheme.

Ruck set Henry Tingay up, then left him dangling with no communication. Tingay was the third plaintiff ordered to pay costs with me, the first plaintiff.

Wayne Peterman was kept "informed," I believe, by both Ruck and Rathdowney. It is glaringly apparent that either Ruck or Rathdowney rang Wayne Peterman on the night before the hearing to inform him of my decision to represent myself.

Peterman, together with Ruck, sold me out and withdrew on the day of the hearing (or the night before), through advice from Sean Ruck's phone call to the courtroom.

Wayne Peterman was the second plaintiff, and initially, in the first order handed down by the DCJ Quincy, Peterman was to pay costs with me. Tingay as the third plaintiff was initially exempt from costs.

Within two hours of the first order being posted, the judge amended the order due to a "spelling mistake." DCJ Betty Quincy had spelled "second" correctly, but said it was incorrect, and it should have spelled "third." So now Peterman was off the hook, and they collared Henry Tingay for half the costs. And now Her Honour and the judge's boy associate know how to spell "third." You be the judge!

I can only assume that Wayne Peterman contacted either Ruck or Rathdowney, for them to contact the judge's boy associate to have the order altered.

It was a can of worms indeed. I have never since had contact with Peterman, who has never volunteered information about his stance and actions regarding our claim and that day I faced court. Peterman was now also a solicitor and part of the cloistered lot. Wayne Peterman had revealed to me that he viewed my submission to the Queensland Law Society, way back when. Peterman had made this Freudian slip by stating he had seen my submission to the QLS while studying for his law degree. I know this to be a lie, bulldust, because the Queensland Law Society will not give out details of a complaint, and the files of the QLS are neither accessible by the public nor students of law.

The only way Wayne Peterman could have perused my complaint submission about Rathdowney, held by only the QLS at the time, was to have read the copy that Rathdowney was sent by Frank Davidson, trust accounts investigator, of the Queensland Law Society at the time.

Peterman had taken to soliciting like a duck to water, embracing the first rule with fever and passion: "Don't ever tackle an anointed one, don't ever apologise, and avoid the truth at all costs."

Wayne Peterman was akin to Norton's Labor buddies. "When the dark storm clouds grew, you chose to desert me, not one phone call, not one visit, no voice of support." So be it.

With all the material gathered from the e-courts' website, the district and supreme courts' registries, I believed the last roll of the dice was through my local member of parliament, Vladimir Rossi, to the senate for a federal executive review.

Hence my affidavit and submission put to the member of parliament, Vladimir Rossi.

As the story has been told, the MP, Vladimir Rossi, passed it to Senator Bill Gillard, a gun barrister. Between both, they sat on my affidavit for nine months before "excusing" themselves, Bill saying, "It's not my jurisdiction."

The two are both seen by me as part of the Queensland connection.

The high court had irreverently disregarded my appeal as an unrepresented appellant. The Queensland connection had by cohesion reached the lofty heights of the High Court of Australia. All this was unbeknown to me at the time, which later added to my existential anxiety.

And His Honour Kerry Pane, on the Queensland Supreme Court of Appeal's bench at the time, was in "transition" of being promoted to the Australian High Court.

The High Court of Australia Special Leave Dispositions reads:

JAN ERNEST GAINSWORTHY
V
HENRY TINGAY & ORS

1. In June 1990 the applicant was introduced to a financial scheme, in which the respondents were also involved. On 15 May 2007 the applicant, together with the first and second respondents ("the plaintiffs"), commenced proceedings against the third respondent in the District Court of Queensland.
2. On 20 March 2009, the District Court Judge heard an application by the third respondent, to strike out the plaintiffs' claim and amended statement of claim, or alternatively for summary judgement. The applicant was the only plaintiff that appeared at the hearing. In March 2009, the District Court Judge entered judgement in favour of the third \respondent. Her honour held that that the equitable defence of laches was a complete defence to the applicant's equitable claim. Her Honour was not satisfied that the applicant's reasons for the delay of almost 18 years in commencing proceedings were

convincing. Her Honour found the third respondent would be considerably prejudiced by the delay.

3. On the 14 June 2009 the applicant sought leave to appeal the Queensland Court of Appeal. On 2 November 2009, the Bench of the Supreme Court refused the application for leave to appeal. The Court of Appeal held that the only arguable ground of appeal concerned the District Court Judge's application of s 27(1) of the *Limitations and Action Act 1974 (Q) ("the Act")*, which provides an exception to a limitation period prescribed by the Act in case of fraud by a trustee. The Court of Appeal held that the District Court Judge was correct that, as the applicant's claim was equitable; his delay precluded the success of his claim despite s 27(1). The Court of Appeal also held the inference drawn by the District Court Judge that the applicant's allegation of fraud was a recent invention raised in an attempt to bring s 27(1) into operation, was open to Her Honour.

4. The applicant seeks leave to appeal this Court. His draft notice of appeal repeats arguments that were addressed by the Court of Appeal and found to be without merit. The draft notice of appeal also alleges that the Court of Appeal exhibited bias and denied the applicant procedural fairness.

5. The applicant has not advanced any questions of law that would justify a grant of special leave to appeal. There are insufficient prospects of success on any appeal to this Court, and there is no reason to doubt the correctness of the Court of Appeal's decision. Special leave is refused.

6. Pursuant to r 41.10.5 we direct the Registrar to draw up, sign and seal an order dismissing the application.

The handing down of this order by two justices of the High Court of Australia, Their Honours Gorbachev and Kyte, serves to illustrate how those in high places can twist the truth to fit their erroneous interpretation of the written law. Kyte was a Queenslander too.

It is a sheer sleight of hand act and aberration to protect the outrageous manipulation of the contorted truth by the lower courts, Rathdowney, Douglas, Black, Ruck, and Abbott. DCJ Quincy's inference that I first alleged fraud eighteen years later is an out-and-out lie. Also, it is an insult to my intelligence and the village idiot's intelligence for those learned ladies and gentlemen of the bar to think that I, and so too the village idiot, would swallow such crap!

The district court judge, Betty Quincy, "inferred" I invented fraud to bring into play s 27(1) of the Limitations of Actions Act.

Again, I did not invent fraud; it's been around forever, it seems. And to "infer" is a personal judgement. For Her Honour to infer, from supposedly the defence's argument, is the twisting of the rules I exposed. It would be on the Brisbane CIB telephone records that I made the complaint of fraud against Rathdowney in 1993. So, by the courts' ignoring my pleading of fraud, I have been denied natural justice.

And tell me how, how would the third respondent, Joe Noel Rathdowney, be considerably prejudiced by this fabrication of delay?

There was no delay on my part! Even if there had been a delay, it is of no consequence, because fraud by a trustee, as Joe Rathdowney was/is, has no statute of time limitation. Refer to s 27(1) of the Limitations of Actions Act. It is axiomatic that every court has erred at law. Every judge and justice have held up Cameron Douglas, SC's defence for the defendant, of "laches" being a complete defence, as Lord Diplock so succinctly stated in another case: "So outrageous in its defence of logic or accepted moral standards that no sensible person who had applied his mind to the question to be decided could have arrived at it."

Yet these learned ladies and gentlemen have allowed one of their own to distort the truth, tarnish the system, and bring about a perversion of natural justice, to further allow another of their own to escape the consequences of committing a crime. What is a reasonable person to think?

By their written law, to pervert or attempt to pervert the course of justice is, in itself a crime, a jailable offence. Ruck and Douglas have also been excused by the system and have not been brought to account for their crimes. They have seemingly been ordained by the anointed ones, excused from taking responsibility for the actions of the choices they made over my life.

I am the one in several billion on this earth plane who selfishly cares about that!

I find it extraordinary that everyone has perjured themselves to save one crooked lawyer who defrauded me and others. I am astounded, dismayed, and, as I say, despondent that these highly intelligent, learned ladies and gentlemen have not had the courage to say, "Stop! Let's put it right."

Stop the madness. It is a lie that snowballed and is now a locomotive out of control. All watching having no chance now of stopping this runaway train. The Queensland Law Society could have nipped it in the bud as early as 1993 and saved many, many red faces—and changed the fate of their karmic wheel.

The Queensland CIB division of police could well have made Rathdowney account for funds released from his firm's trust. It is the law, under the Trust Act, to account in writing within fourteen days, for *any* funds released from a trust! Now it will be played out as karma for all, a train wreck indeed.

My story will be digitally on record indefinitely. Someone may one day put the puzzle together and know of whom I am talking. Surely those in the saga will identify themselves. But I am unsure if any will be embarrassed or be remorseful.

I have heard that the Devil does not do shame or guilt.

The MP Rossi and Senator Gillard would know all the players, as they were provided with every detail. The MP and the senator are now seen by me as in the loop: Queenslanders protecting their own.

These words on the pages of this book represent for me the end, a death to this hideous betrayal over something as temporal as money. Everybody I have approached for help has sold me out, or I have had insufficient funds to buy my justice. So be it.

Death to me is the leveller. All my projected outcomes have been razed to the ground. In hindsight, I had been from pillar to post. All is well. RIP, Tobjoano.

CHAPTER 12

Death the Leveller

Death eventually comes to us all. There is no need to worry, or hurry. All is well and divinely orchestrated. Take the time to stop and smell the flowers, because time and life are so precious a present.

The beginning of this life is being born into time. The ending for this life is signalled by the death of our bodies, the earthly vehicles. However, the human soul is eternal and so are deeds in this lifetime. Be aware and beware: there are no secrets.

Does anyone remember being born?

Einstein's personal take on his own inevitable death is worthy of quoting here: "To one bent on age, death will come as a release. I feel this quite strongly now that I have grown old myself and have come to regard death as an old debt, at long last to be discharged."

There are only a few ways human beings can come to grips with death and understand, from a belief perspective, what death actually means.

From the distorted view of the atheist, death is final. There is no need of last rights or to make amends to a maker or God. The atheist says, "That was my life, and I did what I did." End of story for the atheist.

The Buddhists believe in reincarnation and that what you do in this life determines what you will come back as in the next life. If in this life you were seen as bad, then in the next life you may come back as a rat. "Nonsense," say I, yet I do believe in their attitude of everlasting spiritual life and reincarnation.

I was studying the Chinese language at one time, and my Chinese teacher introduced me to a Buddhist monk who had come out to Australia to study English.

The monk and I had limited success with communication because both of us were beginners in our new languages. However, the look and the body language said it all to me when I took a swipe at a gnat flying around the kitchen table. The monk was aghast that I had tried to kill something that he believed could have been human in the past life. Nonsense. I missed anyway.

The Christian take on death is a little short on how it is too. For shallow believers, their belief is fear based. What they think happens is that you die and wait in line, under the ground or scattered in ashes, for Judgement Day. Judgement Day is the day you meet the maker, and he/she directs you to heaven or hell according to your life lived on this flat Earth and the deeds you have done.

Many think God is not watching and all they need do is 'fess up just before death'. Taking last rites will absolve you of all the sins and entitle you to a first-class ticket to heaven.

I am unsure how Islam interprets death. I believe they relate to death with very much the same understanding as the Christians; that is, there exists heaven and hell.

For all us mortals, it is finished. We cry and mourn for those taken; we pray for our departed and for their souls to rest in peace.

"You're a long time dead" is a common belief.

I have been reticent to say more for fear that I will be labelled a geek or religious. However, Christ Jesus said, "Follow Me, and let the dead bury their own dead." Why did Jesus say, "Let the dead bury their own dead?" This question is a further handful of grist for your mill.

A timely feature article in the *Weekend Australian* magazine by Adam Turner, whom I highly regard as a wordsmith, deals with the topic eloquently. The article was titled "The Bright Side of Death."

I have transcribed excerpts from the last two paragraphs of Turner's article.

If we didn't die, the world would be more crowded and the traffic even worse. If we didn't die, life would not only lose its energy but its poetry.

And, yes, the gift of love.

But I am thinking of something else.

Laughter. Humour comes from knowing about death – and is the best way to deal with it. We come into life with a yell. We can choose to live it – and leave it – with a laugh.

Through my life experiences, I concur with Turner's understanding and expression of life and death. I too can categorically say there is a living God, joy and laughter, the one authority on this flat plane Earth.

The crucifixion and death of the only Son of God, Christ Jesus, was the greatest leveller of all. Yet it was not a sacrifice, as many believe. Jesus did not sacrifice his life. It was God's ransom for our sins. Christ merely was following the will of the Father, to save lives and the worldly plane.

Jesus taught us that there is no death, for Christ overcame the world and death, and lives today. Nobody needs to wait until death's door to contact the Lord. All you need is the faith and a little trust, "as large as a mustard seed." Christ's words live on.

Jesus taught us the Lord's Prayer, which is not supplication, but truly, what we need say to God from the heart, through the Christ Jesus. Remember too we get everything we ask for. Every prayer is heard but only answered when in alignment. The Spirit has no sense of humour and delivers all. You are to intercede on your own behalf, without pleading for intervention.

In Luke 11:2–4 are the words Jesus spoke when teaching his disciples how to pray.

My own version of the Lord's Prayer is as follows:

> Our Father, Mother, God who art in Heaven
> Hallowed and Holy is your Name
> Let your Kingdom come, and
> Your will of love be done, in and through us
> Give us each day our daily bread, and
> Teach us to forgive ourselves, as we forgive others.

> Deliver us from the illusions of the ego, for
> only Your Will is loving and true
> Forever and ever, so be it.
> Amen

Forgiveness is truly the big one. You must firstly forgive yourself for believing you were ever separated from God.

You and I were created equal to all other beings in the eyes of God, on Mother Earth. Mother Earth is a truly magnificent living organism. She is the Yin of the Yang, Father Sky (heaven). Together they are the one, inseparable. There is always yin in yang and, conversely, yang in yin. We are all godly, gifted with individual talents that create the illusion of being different and separated. It follows that the sum of the whole is greater than any individual or group.

The anointed ones have ignored this golden tenet and believe they are above the creator's rules.

Existence is about collaboration, not competitiveness. By way of Chinese whisper, the word *complete* was distorted when passed down the line; it was misinterpreted as *compete*. We are here to complete our lives, not to compete with one another. And no man is an island.

It was said by Albert Einstein, "If you want to live a happy life, tie it to a goal, not to people or objects."

Many instructions have gone awry. I believe that the greatest commandment of all has been ignored. My understanding is that God is still pissed off with the worldly order. If it were not for his only Son, then we all would be smitten by the hand of the Father. This is the true reason we praise the Lord.

Without Jesus's act of supreme benevolence and kindness to come to save mankind, none of us or the world would be here. Do not under any circumstance mistake Christ's kindness as a sign of weakness.

God of course is love, but God without a doubt was pissed off back then by mankind and this weary world, over two thousand years ago. So, God sent his only Son in the flesh to clean it up.

I will paraphrase Abe Lincoln: God doesn't take sides, but we need to know for sure that we have chosen to be on God's side.   Andthis can only be accomplished according to Christ's words, written by his disciple John in his gospel, chapter 14, verse 6: "Jesus said to Thomas, 'I am the way and the truth and the Life; no one comes to the Father except by (through) Me.'"

I have in my possession a black-and-white reproduction of an actual photograph of Sananda, taken on 1 June 1961, in Chechen Itza, Yucatán, by Dr Steinbeck, one of thirty archaeologists working in the area at that time.

Sananda appeared in a visible, tangible body and permitted his photograph to be taken. (The source and time of acquisition of the photograph is unknown.)

Of all the lessons I have learned by going through this Tobjoano offshore loans ordeal, surely the fact that I stumbled upon God and truth was the greatest and most rewarding. It is a gift that money cannot buy, and no one can take from me. Jesus is the truth and the life; there justice can be found. Christ is one with the Father. Together with the Spirit, they are the Trinity, the one authority on earth.

Einstein, the man of the twentieth century, gave this reply, when asked about God and religion: "Try and penetrate with our limited means the secrets of Nature and you will find that; behind all the discernible concatenations, there remains something subtle, intangible and inexplicable. Veneration for this force beyond anything we can comprehend is my religion."

When asked by a journalist, "What's it like being the smartest man on earth?" Einstein replied, "I don't know, you need to ask Nikola Tesla."

The good news is that it is a never-ending story. God's love makes the Sun go around the world, not money.

Einstein's view of the world and peace is insightful and could well be applied to my worldly experiences of Tobjoano and prejudice dealt me by legal system over the time. Einstein said of peace, "The ancient Jehovah is still abroad, he slays the innocent along with the guilty, whom he strikes so fearsomely blind that they can feel no sense of guilt ... We are dealing with an epidemic delusion which having caused infinite suffering that will one day vanish and become a monstrous and incomprehensible source of wonderment to later generations."

If all the money in the world dried up, then the world would still remain stationary, protected by the firmament and life would not be extinguished. However, if God's love were to stop flowing, the Son would cease giving light and warmth; you would have approximately nine seconds to drop your pants, put your head between your knees, and to kiss your arse goodbye.

It's over. Laugh out loud.

Stick with my programme by adopting the attitude of gratitude; live and let live.

Keep the faith and be kind to yourself. Say often to those in your sphere of influence, "All is well."

"Love, light, and laughter" is my salutation.

Apply the KISS principle to every situation: keep it simple, sweetheart.

Jan Ernest Gainsworthy

I had been sailing, pointed close to the wind, for over twenty years. At the funeral of Steven R., in my imagination, I heard the Captain give the command, "Ready about Jan."

EPILOGUE

Deadlines are a healthy part of existence. If it weren't for deadlines, "stuff" would go on ad infinitum. Life would become boring, with no new avenues of expression—a "same stuff, different day" mindset.

The end to a play is conventionally signalled by the fat lady singing. And, with the chorus, "it's time to pay the piper".

I have been aware of neither signal to wind up proceedings. My only prompt was the vivid image of the final curtain as it was closing on Stephen R.'s coffin.

That moment terminated the worry and struggle of this saga. "Moneys owing" is simply not worth dying for. Life is too short to hang on to old patterns, for it is the old patterns that impede the progress of all.

Crossing your bridges in life and reaching for the unreachable star is the attitude one should adopt and strive to live by. Onward and upward, doggedly, toward heaven is the edict. Apply lavishly the attitude of gratitude.

I suggest you burn your bridges, so you can't go back. Leave the dross behind; look to a brighter future. Have the courage and faith to follow your heart's desire.

"Are you doing the dream, Gainsworthy?" A question that a good friend, Sami, challenged me with.

No words were exchanged, just a smile and a warm glow of understanding. In real time, it was another pointer to say, "Enough, Jan, enough!"

Goals are chosen but your purpose is discovered. By constantly re-evaluating and aligning your goals, life's never-ending story unfolds. The journey is not half of it—the journey is all of it. But take some time to stop and smell the flowers along the way. Become aware of the present moment and adopt the attitude of gratitude. Say often to those in your sphere of influence, "All is indeed well."

Everyone has a story to tell of their journeys along the royal red road travelled on this flat earth. Stories of the hurdles jumped, the bridges crossed, the stony tracks traversed, and the mountains climbed. We take the good and expunge the bad as much as possible. When crossing those bridges, keep your goals from your trolls!

Do not tell the trolls guarding those bridges of your dreams. To keep silent is the fourth rule of wisdom. Some give up on their dreams; in turn, they give up on life. "Never, ever give up" is the decree.

There are four rules to wisdom:

1. To know,
2. To will,
3. To dare,
4. And the forth rule, most often broken, is to keep silent. (Don't tell the trolls.)

Another decree from the one authority on earth is to become childlike, not childish.

Through the two listeners, back in 1935, who channelled Christ's instruction and produced a little daily devotional book, *God Calling*, Jesus said:

> Seek in every way to become child-like. Seek, seek, seek until you find, until the years have added to your nature that of a trusting child. Not only for its simple trust that you must copy the child-spirit, but for its joy in life, its ready laughter, its lack of criticism, its desire to share with all men. Ask much that you may become as little children, friendly and loving toward all—not critical, not fearful.

"Except ye become as little children ye cannot enter the Kingdom of Heaven."

Those words are similar to what was said in regard to the difficulty for a rich man being able to go through the eye of a needle or pass to heaven. You cannot buy a ticket to heaven; you must earn the right of passage. It is something money cannot secure, though many have tried to bargain.

I admonish my audience to take each day at a time. Give thanks for your existence each day and expect miracles to unfold. Worry not of tomorrow, because time only exists in the now, and the now is the present.

Yes! ... A present! It is an unconditional gift, which is given freely from the one authority on earth.

Blessings already are!

APPENDIX I

Two prayers that have seen me through this sordid saga are the Serenity Prayer and the Lord's Prayer. I suggest that in the trials and tribulations of life pertaining to human existence, one must rest at difficult stations and be still before continuing the journey. In a similar fashion, the Boy Scouts are taught that if one becomes lost in the wilderness, first stop and get one's bearings before advancing.

With calm mindfulness, empty your heart of hatred and revenge. Having no expectations nor pleadings, recite these powerful words of prayer.

In time, the answer comes for the understanding of any situation. And too, give thanks and praise to the one authority on earth. Justice.

The Serenity Prayer

God grant me the serenity to accept the things I cannot change;
The courage to change the things I can change;
And the wisdom to know the difference.

Desiderata

My own version of the Lord's Prayer

Our Father, Mother, God who art in Heaven
Hallowed and Holy is your Name
Let your Kingdom come, and
Your will of love be done, in and through us
Give us each day our daily bread, and the fulfilment of our needs
Teach us to forgive ourselves, as we forgive others.
Deliver us from the illusions of the ego, for
only Your Will is loving and true
Forever and ever, so be it.
Amen

ACKNOWLEDGEMENTS

Aunt Evelyn is truly a shining light. I acknowledge her everlasting trust in Christ Jesus, and her prayers, together with her earthly endeavours to promote my submission.

To Aunt Evelyn I say, "Many thanks indeed." I am humbled and deeply grateful.

Xie xie Nin,
Jan Ernest Gainsworthy

I acknowledge my elder brother, Maxwell, for his willing contribution in editing the first book, *Without Prejudice: Nailing the Standard.*

Without Max's scrutiny in honing the very rough draft in the early days, there would be little chance of a polished and finished publication. Much of Maxwell's coaching and instruction has been carried across to this sequel, *Those in Ivory Towers: Lawmakers Lawbreakers.* The initial editing work lessened the stresses of achieving an acceptable copy. Thank you, Max.

To all the players who have made my story real: I acknowledge you, but there are no warm and fuzzy embraces, nor is there a thank-you. "Have a nice life."

I too acknowledge my American publisher, Xlibris for steering the author through the treacherous waters of book publishing. It has been a profoundly exciting and rewarding experience; guided by remarkable professionals that deserve recognition as co-authors, especially the editor, a genius! Sincerely, thank you.

To all those that have come and gone before me, those who have not hidden their lamps under bushels: I salute you, for you have blazed a trail for future generations (my grandchildren) to follow. It is a trail lit by a beacon of impeccable faith and trust of the one authority.

Last but by no means least, I acknowledge the Infinite Intelligence. That which whom has strung the stars in the night sky and the wondering stars in the heavens, father sky and created mother earth, protected by a dome, separating the waters above from the waters below.

An unconditional love; a knowing that protects and guides through stormy waters.

"All is indeed well."
True justice persists.
There is only one authority on earth.

2018-six-years later, there will be a next book, of the trilogy. Never say never!

www.ingramcontent.com/pod-product-compliance
Lightning Source LLC
Chambersburg PA
CBHW030748180526
45163CB00003B/944